T0368099

STATISTICALLY SIGNIFICANT

The Science of Jesus as the Son of God

Tim Mack, Ph.D.

WESTBOW
P R E S S®
A DIVISION OF THOMAS NELSON
& ZONDERVAN

WestBow Press books may be ordered through booksellers or by contacting:

WestBow Press
A Division of Thomas Nelson & Zondervan
1663 Liberty Drive
Bloomington, IN 47403
www.westbowpress.com
844-714-3454

ISBN: 979-8-3850-3913-5 (sc)
ISBN: 979-8-3850-3912-8 (e)

Print information available on the last page.

WestBow Press rev. date: 02/14/2025

Book Review

In "Statistically Significant: The Science of Jesus As The Son of God," Dr. Tim Mack presents a compelling exploration of the divine nature of Jesus Christ through a rigorous scientific lens. This book is a testament to the power of blending faith with empirical analysis, offering readers a robust framework for understanding the miraculous claims of Christianity.

Dr. Mack employs a meticulous scientific approach to document his conclusions, underpinned by irrefutable evidence drawn from a diverse range of sources. The use of the scientific method not only enhances the credibility of his arguments but also showcases a well tested, systematic approach that reinforces the validity of his findings.

One of the standout features of this work is its integration of recorded scripture with established customs from both the Old and New Testaments. This correlation adds a valuable dimension to the discussion, providing a deeper understanding and validation of the scriptural authenticity that Dr. Mack seeks to affirm.

The section on "Mathematical Experiment" is particularly noteworthy. Dr. Mack adeptly demonstrates the mathematical probability of Old Testament prophecies coming to fruition in the New Testament. This mathematical analysis serves as a powerful faith-building tool, offering a unique and convincing argument for the divine nature of these prophecies.

Dr. Mack's thorough background information on the original sources, who were esteemed scholars and authorities in their time, further enriches the reader's experience. By correlating these authorities with the scriptural passages in The Bible, Dr. Mack aligns historical scholarship with theological claims, enhancing the book's authority and persuasiveness.

Christ Jesus's words, "Blessed are those who have not seen and believe," resonate throughout the text. Dr. Mack's work is designed to strengthen belief and faith through careful reflection and internalization of his well-organized, logical arguments. The book is accessible and structured in a way that allows readers to arrive at Dr. Mack's conclusions with clarity and minimal skepticism.

The final section of the book serves as a practical guide for both believers and skeptics. It offers valuable resources and time-tested suggestions for those looking to deepen their faith or explore Christianity further. The practical advice is both actionable and easy to follow, making it a helpful tool for anyone seeking to understand or trust in Christ as their savior.

In summary, "Statistically Significant: The Science of Jesus As The Son of God" is a masterful and comprehensive work that is highly recommended for both believers and non-believers. Whether you are curious about the intersection of science and faith or seeking affirmation of your beliefs, Dr. Mack's book provides a thoughtful and persuasive examination of Jesus's divine nature.

John R. Johnson
Church Planter & Pastor, and retired Associate Dean for Teacher Education
Grace Bible Chapel

Contents

Dedication

This book is dedicated to my lovely wife, Linda Jane Lee Mack, and our children, Rebecca, Rachel, Amanda, Brian, and Joseph. They are a daily shining light in my life. Linda has been the love of my life for 48 years (and counting!). I am grateful for the love and support of my wife and family.

Introduction

If you ask people today what they think of 'science,' you'll get mixed reactions. Some might reply that science has disproved God. It hasn't. Others might say that they don't trust science anymore. Science asks questions and answers them objectively. Science isn't biased and doesn't spin an answer to fit dogma or politics. Unfortunately, we often see scientists, who are as fallible as the rest of us, fall short of these attributes. Science is informative when used correctly.

What does science tell us about Jesus? We can examine historical, archeological, medical, geological, astronomical, prophetic, and even mathematical data about Jesus' life, death, and resurrection. I analyzed data for years as a research scientist, so I used science to study the data for Jesus as the Son of God. The science says that Jesus is the Son of God.

PART ONE reviews how the biblical text has been passed down to us. It includes a discussion of Iranaeus, Polycarp, the Codex Sinaiticus, and the exacting nature of Hebrew scribes. PART TWO reviews archeological data related to Jesus' life, such as the Pool of Siloam, Caiaphas' ossuary, James' ossuary, one of Herod's fortresses, and other findings. PART THREE shows that Jesus was brutally tortured and died, most likely from a heart attack caused by hypovolemic shock. It documents an earthquake when Jesus died and proves that the darkness was not an ordinary solar eclipse. It also shows that Jesus' body wasn't stolen. Part FOUR presents evidence that Jesus rose from the dead and the citizens of Jerusalem weren't fooled by an 'imposter Jesus.' PART FIVE lists 25 Old Testament prophecies that Jesus fulfilled and statistically calculates that there is <u>less than one in 33 million</u> chance that all 25 prophecies were fulfilled by other events such as random chance, nature, etc. This minuscule probability means those prophecies were fulfilled by Jesus instead of other events. He is the Son of God.

PART SIX recommends what to do next as a new Christian, such as how to find a good church and why it's essential to believe the entire Bible (e.g., don't believe in false prophets or Prosperity Theology).

Let's begin!

PART 1: HISTORICAL DATA

The New Testament books record Jesus' life and death, so it makes sense to begin here. Are these documents data? Yes. We can see an ancient document because someone wrote something and someone else 'collected' it. We can compare accounts from several authors and ones not in the New Testament to look for consistency. Data that don't match are a problem in science.

Was the New Testament Copied Accurately?

The New Testament has first-person eyewitnesses to Jesus Christ's ministry and resurrection. The Apostles talked, ate, and traveled with Jesus. They saw his persecution, and John saw Jesus on the cross. These Apostles

FROM: Wikimedia Commons: Rev Robert Traill's New Testament (1656).jpg

also saw and spoke to a risen Jesus. Then, they wrote this down for us to read.

Their thoughts have been passed down to us for over 1,900 years, and we must know that we are reading what they wrote and not something that has been embellished, miscopied, or just made into a fairy tale. Let's explore how these critical texts have been passed on to us.

TRANSMITTAL OF BIBLICAL DATA OVER TIME

The first step is to see if the data about Jesus were accurately transmitted to others over time. J. Warner Wallace, who authored the 2013 book, 'Cold-Case Christianity,' uses an analogy of how a crime must have an untainted chain of custody to ensure the evidence wasn't tampered with.

This is also true for data, which cannot be allowed to be corrupted. I was an entomologist who studied insects that attacked certain field crops, and the insects could destroy hundreds of millions of dollars of crops in a single year. We did field, greenhouse, and laboratory experiments. Members of my research program collected hundreds to thousands of lines of data each year on data sheets. These sheets were formatted for the specific experiment and required the user to write down specific information about the date, time, location, sample number, and number and kind of arthropods counted.

The information was entered into a computer so that we could statistically analyze the data. One person did data entry, and each entry was checked to verify its fidelity. We then used a statistical package to produce some basic plots and tables, partially as another way to confirm that someone entered the data correctly.

We also used remote monitors for experiments where a computer checked a sensor network and transmitted data to us. We reviewed the electronic transmittal to see if the computer sent us all the data.

Using this approach, we need to know that:

- There is a clear trail of data transmission.
- Other sources match the data, so there aren't any anomalies.

PERSON-TO-PERSON DATA TRANSMISSION

A 'disciple-to-student' transfer of information about Jesus occurred over several hundred years, and those men all describe Jesus' crucifixion and resurrection. Dr. Kenneth Calvert, from Hillsdale College, offers an excellent online course[1] entitled 'Ancient Christianity' that discusses Polycarp, Irenaeus, Hippolytus, Ignatius, Tertullian, Origen, Augustine, and others. J.

---

[1] Lesson 5: Calvert, K. 2024. Apostles, Creed, and Scripture. In 'Ancient Christianity.' https://online.hillsdale.edu

Warner Wallace also discusses several famous church fathers in that list.[2] I focus on Polycarp, Irenaeus, and Hippolytus. For example, we have the Apostle John (died ca. 98 A.D.[3]) having Polycarp (died ca. 160 A.D.[4]) as a disciple, and Polycarp had Irenaeus (died 202 A.D.[5]) as a disciple. Hippolytus (died 235 A.D.[6]) was a famous contemporary of Irenaeus. Who were these clergy?

POLYCARP: He lived from 69-160 A.D. and was a disciple of the Apostle John. Polycarp became the Bishop of Smyrna. Irenaeus related these thoughts about Polycarp, *"I seem to hear him now relate how he conversed with John and many others who had seen Jesus Christ, the words he had heard from their mouths."* [7] Polycarp was in his 80s when he became at loggerheads with the Roman Proconsul. Polycarp was allegedly offered a chance to recant by saying, 'Caesar is Lord,' and he refused. So, he was burned at the stake. Legend has it that the flames didn't kill

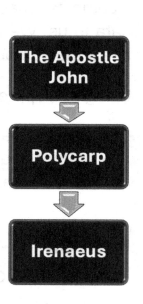

[2] https://coldcasechristianity.com/writings/
four-reasons-the-new-testament-gospels-are-reliable/
[3] https://www.gotquestions.org/apostle-John-die.html
[4] https://christianhistoryinstitute.org/study/module/polycarp/
[5] https://www.gotquestions.org/Irenaeus-of-Lyons.html
[6] https://en.wikipedia.org/wiki/Hippolytus_of_Rome
[7] https://www.bartehrman.com/polycarp/

him; a Roman then stabbed him with a spear. There is an excellent 2015 movie about Polycarp; it is currently on tubitv.com. Polycarp is a saint today in the Roman Catholic Church and others.

IRENAEUS: He lived from 170-202 A.D. and was a disciple of Polycarp. Irenaeus became the Bishop of Lugdunum in Gaul (Lyon in modern France) in 178 A.D. Today, he is known as Irenaeus of Lyon.[8] Amongst other works, he wrote 'Proof of Apostolic Preaching.'[9] Irenaeus is best known for his emphasis on Jesus's humanity. A quote from Irenaeus about Jesus' crucifixion is, *"God forbid that I should glory in anything save in the cross of Christ, by whom the world is crucified to me, and I unto the world."*[10] No one knows how Irenaeus died, but he could have been martyred. The Roman Catholic Church canonized him.

HIPPOLYTUS OF ROME: He lived from about 170-235 A.D. and was a contemporary of Irenaeus. Hippolytus was a prolific writer of Christian thought. He was an elder of the church in Rome and was a brilliant theologian. Most scholars view his 'Refutation of All Heresies'[11] as his most important work. As one would expect, Hippolytus wrote about Jesus and his

---

[8] https://www.gotquestions.org/Irenaeus-of-Lyons.html

[9] https://www.christian-history.org/apostolic-preaching-intro-irenaeus.html

[10] http://www.earlychristianwritings.com/text/irenaeus-book1.html

[11] http://www.ancienttexts.org/library/celtic/ctexts/classical_hippolytus.html

crucifixion. For example, *"Do not the Romans rule the country? And indeed these impious people hated thee, and did saw thee asunder, and they crucified Christ. Thou art dead in the world, but thou livest in Christ."*[12]

OTHER SOURCES OF DATA

Let's examine data from ancient historians, an ancient copy of the Bible, and the Dead Sea Scrolls. At least two historically significant historians discuss Jesus and ancient Israel: Flavius Josephus and Eusebius of Caesarea.

FLAVIUS JOSEPHUS: He was a Jewish writer who lived from about 32-100 A.D., making him a contemporary of the Apostles. He was born in Jerusalem and participated in the Jewish Rebellion of 66 A.D. Josephus was captured and became a slave of General Titus.[13] This General gave Josephus his freedom when Titus became Emperor.

Josephus wrote, amongst others:

- 'Wars of the Jews,' ca. 75 A.D.
- 'Antiquities of the Jews,' ca. 94 A.D.

---

[12] http://www.earlychristianwritings.com/text/hippolytus-christ.html
[13] https://en.wikipedia.org/wiki/Josephus

Josephus is an excellent source for understanding the Maccabean Revolt, led by Judas 'The Hammer' Maccabeus in 167-160 B.C. This revolt occurred between the Old and New Testaments and is interesting to Christians.

Josephus wrote about James, the brother of Jesus: *"...so he assembled the sanhedrim [sic] of judges, and brought before them the brother of Jesus, who was called Christ, whose name was James, and some others, [or, some of his companions]; and when he had formed an accusation against them as breakers of the law, he delivered them to be stoned..."*[14] In this verse, we read that Jesus' brother James was brought before the Sanhedrin, Jerusalem's ruling body of religious leaders.

Josephus also wrote about Jesus in his 'Antiquities of the Jews' series, book 3, section 3, *"Now there was about this time Jesus, a wise man, if it be lawful to call him a man; for he was a doer of wonderful works, a teacher of such men as receive the truth with pleasure...He was [the] Christ. And when Pilate, at the suggestion of the principal men amongst us, had condemned him to the cross, those that loved him at the first did not forsake him; for he appeared to them alive again the third day; as the divine prophets*

---

[14] Complete Works and Historical Background (Annotated and Illustrated) (Annotated Classics) by Flavius Josephus. https://a.co/d7fV6RQ

had foretold these and ten thousand other wonderful things concerning him." These data from <u>outside the Bible</u> show that Jesus died and was crucified.

EUSEBIUS OF CAESAREA: Eusebius was a Greek historian of early Christianity who lived from about 260-339 A.D. Scholars believe that Eusebius lived in or around Caesarea Maritima, on the coast of the eastern Mediterranean. He became the Bishop of Caesarea Maritima in 314 A.D. Eusebius wrote 40 books, and his book, 'The History of the Church From the Time of Christ to the Conversion of Constantine,' is the best known. Eusebius is sometimes called, 'The Father of Church History.'[15] He used quotes from primary sources that would otherwise have been lost to us, which makes his writings quite valuable.

Eusebius wrote extensively about Jesus. For example, *"Then, finally, at the time of the origin of the Roman Empire, there appeared again to all men and nations throughout the world, who had been, as it were, previously assisted, and were now fitted to receive the knowledge of the Father, that same teacher of virtue, the minister of the Father in all good things, the divine and heavenly Word of God, in a human body not at all differing in substance from our own. He did and suffered the things which had been prophesied...The marvelous nature of his birth, and his new teaching, and his wonderful works had also been foretold; so*

---

[15] https://www.gotquestions.org/Eusebius-of-Caesarea.html

likewise the manner of his death, his resurrection from the dead, and, finally, his divine ascension into heaven." This quote attests that Eusebius discussed Jesus's death and resurrection. The Roman Catholic Church venerates Eusebius.

Both these Historians documented Jesus' life and death. Josephus was the earlier Jewish Historian, and Eusebius was the later Greek Historian. Eusebius's life ended about the same time as a later major historical work was written...the Codex Sinaiticus.

THE CODEX SINAITICUS

The next significant event is the Codex Sinaiticus. A Codex is a book and is an advancement over a large and bulky scroll.

FROM: Wikimedia Commons: To Sinai via the Red Sea, Tor, and Wady Hebran. Facsimile of the Codex Sinaiticus [Monastery of St. Catherine].

"The Codex Sinaiticus is one of the most import-ant books in the world. Handwritten well over 1600 years ago, the manuscript contains the Christian Bible in Greek, including the oldest complete copy of the New Testament."[16]

It was written sometime between 300 to 399 A.D.

---

[16] https://codexsinaiticus.org/en/

We can compare modern texts to the Codex Sinaiticus. The fidelity between the Codex Sinaiticus and contemporary New Testament text is remarkable. For example, we can compare the New Testament King James version with the Codex Sinaiticus version of Mark 15:16-21. Below is the King James Version of these verses and the Codex Sinaiticus Version of those verses from the Codex Sinaiticus website.[17]

KING JAMES VERSION: *"And the soldiers led him away into the hall, called Praetorium; and they call together the whole band. And they clothed him with purple, and platted a crown of thorns, and put it about his head, And began to salute him, Hail, King of the Jews! And they smote him on the head with a reed, and did spit upon him, and bowing their knees worshipped him. And when they had mocked him, they took off the purple from him, and put his own clothes on him, and led him out to crucify him. And they compel one Simon a Cyrenian, who passed by, coming out of the country, the father of Alexander and Rufus, to bear his cross."*

CODEX SINAITICUS VERSION:[18] *"And the soldiers led him away within the court, which is the Pretorium, and called together the whole band. And they clothed him in purple, and having plaited a crown of thorns they put it on him: And began to salute him: Hail,*

---

[17] https://codexsinaiticus.org/en/
[18] https://codexsinaiticus.org/en/manuscript.aspx?__VIEWSTATEGENE RATOR=01FB804F&book=34&chapter=16&lid=en&side=r&zoomSlider=0

King of the Jews. And they struck his head with a reed, and spit upon him, and bowing the knees they worshipped him. And when they had derided him, they took off from him the purple, and put on him his own clothes. And they led him out to crucify him, And they impressed one, Simon a Cyrenian, as he passed by coming from the country, the father of Alexander and Rufus, to bear his cross."

The similarity is remarkable, considering that the King James Version was published in 1611, at least 1,200 years after the Codex Sinaiticus.

This uniformity of text over time is also verified by comparing our Bible today with other ancient biblical fragments. Ken Boa says[19] the New Testament *"...can be regarded as 99.5% pure, and the correct readings for the remaining 0.5 percent can often be ascertained with a fair degree of probability by the practice of textual criticism."*

Ken Boa also notes how ancient biblical fragments are dated to the time of Christ, *"The John Rylands Fragment (P52) of the Gospel of John is dated at A.D. 117-38, only a few decades after the Gospel was written. The Bodmer Papyri are dated from A.D. 175-225, and the Chester Beatty Papyri date from about A.D. 250. The time span for most of the New Testament is less than 200 years (and some books are*

---

[19] https://bible.org/article/how-accurate-bible

within 100 years) from the date of authorship to the date of our earliest manuscripts. This can be sharply contrasted with the average gap of over 1,000 years between the composition and the earliest copy of the writings of other ancient authors."

COMPARING THE HISTORICITY OF SOCRATES WITH JESUS

Jesus is often compared with Socrates.[20] Many of us grew up believing that Socrates existed. He was a Greek philosopher who lived in Athens and was executed in 339 B.C. We can compare what we know about Jesus Christ to what we know about Socrates, and this is a good comparison because:

- There is no tomb or body for either Jesus or Socrates.
- Neither wrote a document himself that we know of.

The primary sources for us to know about Socrates are just three people: Aristophanes, Plato, and Xenophon. Aristophanes was a playwright who knew him, and Plato and Xenophon

FROM: Wikimedia Commons: Socrates_ (transparent).png

were his students. Four other ancient writers mentioned Socrates: Antisthenes, Aristippus of Cyrene, Phaedo

---

[20] https://godblog.org/socrates-and-jesus-christ/

of Elis, and Euclid of Megara. None of their writings survive, and their remarks about Socrates are attributed to them in other texts. That's it for actual sources, to the best of my knowledge.

There are fewer than 30 ancient texts that mention Socrates. Do you believe that Socrates exists? If so, then you'll have to believe that Jesus existed because there is much more evidence of that in the ancient copies of the New Testament. If you don't believe in all these copies, you shouldn't believe in any ancient document.

ANCIENT SCRIBES WERE EXACTING TRANSCRIBERS

These ancient copies enable us to compare them against each other and we see conformity in the copies. We expect this if we know the scribes' precise methods of copying Biblical text.

JEWISH SCRIBES (Old Testament): Josh McDowell described the profession of Jewish scribes.[21] They made their ink and used ceremonially clean animal skins. McDowell noted, *"Then came the critical task of ensuring that he copied every letter clearly and straight. Using threads as guides, the scribe took a dull knife that would not cut through the skin and carefully*

---

[21] https://www.josh.org/meticulous-scribes-trusted-manuscript/

scored the surface horizontally. This indented the skin slightly to form a distinguishable line. He repeated the same process vertically, creating a perfect cross-pattern grid on which to copy each and every letter of God's written Word."

In Jewish tradition, the scribe would have uttered each word aloud before writing it down. Scribes were forbidden to write scripture from memory, but they had a copy next to them. A scribe had to memorize several thousand laws about how to copy scripture.

Another scribe checked the copy once it was completed. McDowell writes, *"Some traditions required three separate rabbis to check the accuracy! This meant these persons had to completely unroll this 72-foot scroll to check and count every single word and all 304,805 of the letters. They had to be sure there was the same number of letters in this scroll compared to the Torah from which it was copied. Not only that, when they counted the words, they knew the center word was found in Leviticus 13:33. If the center word of the new scroll did not fall exactly within verse 33, it could not be certified. They did the same thing for every letter. The center letter was found in Leviticus 11:45. If the center letter in the new scroll was in verse 45, they could be confident they had an exact replica of the previous Torah."*

The above procedure is a precise way of copying text, which may explain why scribes apprenticed for years before they could be truly scribes.

GREEK SCRIBES (New Testament): Scribes were valued for writing and preserving documents in the Greco-Roman world at the time of Jesus. Michael A. Freeman noted in his PhD dissertation that Greek scribes also had an apprenticeship.[22] They also underwent years of training in reading, writing, grammar, and rhetoric.

There are over 20,000 handwritten copies of the New Testament in several languages[23] and several million pages of text. Many of these copies weren't made by professional scribes. As a result, there are about 300,000 to 400,000 text variants in those 20,000 copies. These variants could be spelling differences, changes in word order, translation differences, and the addition or omission of words. For example, New Testament scholar Dr. Daniel Wallace noted that the phrase 'John loves Mary' could be written 384 ways in ancient Greek.[24] All 384 mean that John loves Mary, but 383 would be called textual variants. And that is from just a three-word sentence! According to Dr.

---

[22] Freeman, M. 2023. The Hands that Write: Life and Training of Greco-Roman Scribes. Department of Classical Studies, Duke University. 215 pp.

[23] The ESV Study Bible. 2018. Crossway, Wheaton, II.

[24] Is What We Have Now What They Wrote then? https://www.youtube.com/watch?v=n5AKPiBZcis

Wallace, about 99.8% of textual variants <u>don't affect</u> <u>anything</u>, and the doctrinal statements (such as John 14:6) are unchanged. So, we can be confident that the Bible we read has been accurately passed down to us.

THE DEAD SEA SCROLLS PROVE THAT EXACT COPYING OCCURRED

These scrolls show that the Old Testament was copied accurately. They were discovered in the Qumran Caves in Israel beginning in 1947. More than 15,000 scrolls and fragments were found, dating from the 3rd century B.C to the 1st century B.C.

There is a Dead Sea scroll that contains Isaiah 53. Dr. Norman Geisler compared this scroll from 125 B.C. to the modern text of Isaiah 53. He noted, *"Of the 166 words in Isaiah 53, there are only 17 letters in question. Ten of these letters are simply a matter of spelling, which does not affect the sense. Four more letters are minor stylistic changes, such as conjunctions. The remaining three letters comprise the word 'light' which is added in verse 11, and does not affect the meaning greatly."*[25]

There is a 2,100+ year difference between the Dead Sea Scroll version of Isaiah and today's version. Precise copying of the scriptures in the Bible shouldn't

---

[25] https://www.youtube.com/watch?v=8bWojVoCKvk

surprise anyone. The Old and New Testaments have always been Holy texts and were treated with great care in copying. Yes, we can believe the texts were copied accurately and have not been sullied over time.

ARE PROCEDURES IN THE BIBLE ACCURATE?

Another way to assess the fidelity of the New Testament is to see if its procedures match what we know from outside the Bible. J. Warner Wallace noted that procedures mentioned in the New Testament include correct descriptions of Roman citizenship and Roman penal processes.[26] For example, the apostle Paul was a Roman citizen by birth. In contrast, the Roman commander mentioned in Acts 22:28 had to buy his citizenship. Roman citizenship was complex, and several laws and traditional practices governed it. 'The Twelve Tables' is the oldest record of Roman citizenship rights and describes Roman citizens' rights in court proceedings, property, and death.[27] For example, people could complete a public service and obtain Roman citizenship rights; cities could enact Latin law and elect people to public office who became Roman citizens.[28] Military service could lead

---

[26] https://coldcasechristianity.com/writings/
the-case-for-the-reliability-of-the-new-testament-free-bible-insert/
[27] https://en.wikipedia.org/wiki/Twelve_Tables
[28] https://en.wikipedia.org/wiki/Roman_citizenship

to Roman citizenship. Likewise, penal practices were clearly defined in the Twelve Tables, and Paul did have rights as a Roman citizen that were violated.[29]

When Were the Earliest Books of the New Testament Written?

We must also know <u>when</u> the earliest first-person eyewitness accounts of Jesus Christ's ministry and resurrection were written. We ask, *"Were the very first books of the New Testament written soon after Jesus' death or much later?"*

Here is a timeline of events relevant to answering this question:

- ca. 60 A.D. Luke writes Acts (Paul is alive in Acts).
- ca. 62 A.D. James is executed.
- ca. 64-67 A.D. Emperor Nero executes Paul.
- 66 A.D. Jewish revolt begins.
- 70 A.D. The siege and destruction of Jerusalem occurred in April-August by Roman General Titus, who later became Emperor Titus Caesar Vespanius.

---

[29] https://sharperiron.org/article/
apostle-paul-and-his-rights-as-roman-citizen

The Jewish revolt was an effort to throw off the oppression of the Roman Empire. Emperor Nero sent General Vespasian to crush the uprising. Vespasian became Emperor when Nero died, and Vespasian sent his son Titus to capture Jerusalem. He besieged Jerusalem three days before Passover, ensuring that a massive number of people were trapped inside. Jews throughout the Middle East and the Mediterranean journeyed to Jerusalem for Passover, and as many as one million people may have been there. Joachim Jeremias reported that *"...the number of corpses of poor people thrown out through the gates was 600,000..."*[30] What a terrible loss of life!

Some people might say that the number killed should be smaller. Okay, suppose that only half of that number died...300,000 people. That was still an <u>unmitigated disaster</u> for Jews and one that would be remembered. Titus breached the walls in Jerusalem and he ensured that the Second Temple in Jerusalem was destroyed.

Jesus foretold this event: *"The days will come upon you when your enemies will build an embankment against you and encircle you and hem you in on every side. They will dash you to the ground, you and the children within your walls. They will not leave one stone on another, because you did not recognize the time of God's coming to you."* Luke 19:43-44.

---

[30] Jeremias, J. 1969. Excursus The Number of Pilgrims at Passover. IN: Jerusalem in the Time of Jesus. SCM Press Ltd. 495 pp.

The destruction of Jerusalem was a horrific event! The death toll and the destruction of the Temple must have been burned into the hearts and minds of every Jew involved in it. Thousands of people died, and probably more than that fled when this happened.

This traumatic event is so significant that we'd expect Apostles to mention it if they wrote after 70 A.D. The Books of Mark, James, and Luke are some of the earliest known books of the New Testament, so we could see if they mentioned this terrible event.

MARK: Luke most likely wrote his text before the Apostle Paul died, and Luke appears to have used Mark as a source. Therefore, Mark wrote his text as early as 45-50 A.D. If Jesus died in 33 A.D., this would be about 12-17 years after his death, which isn't very long. There is also evidence that this and Matthew's account were written from an earlier creed. The gospel of Mark doesn't mention the destruction of Jerusalem.

JAMES: 'James the Just' was the brother of Jesus and was killed in 62 A.D. James would have written about the destruction of the Second Temple because he was the head of the Christian church in Jerusalem. He did not write about it. The book of James doesn't mention gentiles as Paul's writings do, suggesting that James wrote his text before Paul's epistles. Based on that and the absence of mention of food offered to idols and other 'current topics' that Paul wrote, this book was probably written about 50 A.D.

LUKE: There is a thorough discussion of the date for Luke in crossexamned.org.[31] Luke was Paul's traveling companion and would undoubtedly have mentioned his friend's death. We can be confident that Acts and Luke were written about 62 A.D.[32]

PAUL: The English Standard Version Bible Study Guide estimated that Paul was martyred in Rome between 64-67 A.D by Emperor Nero. Paul wrote Romans, 1 & 2 Corinthians, Galatians, Ephesians, Philippians, Colossians, 1 & 2 Thessalonians, and 1 & 2 Timothy. All these books were written before Paul's death, of course. None mention of the destruction of Jerusalem.

WHY DID THE APOSTLES WAIT TO WRITE SOMETHING?

Knowledge and ideas were passed down orally from one generation to the next in ancient Judea because most people couldn't read.

Oral traditions can be accurate. For example, Jewish listeners would have heard the Old Testament stories all their lives in the synagogue. They would know if someone

[31] https://crossexamined.org/wrote-gospel-luke-acts/
[32] Study Bible, English Standard Version. 2016. Crossway Publishing, Wheaton, IL. Page 1935.

altered a story. Given the oral traditions of the Jewish religion at the time (i.e., singing the Psalms), it seems likely that there was oral testimony that early Christians recited. This would have predated the Gospels.

Lee Strobel wrote in 'The Case for Christ,' *"A good case can be made for saying that Christian belief in the Resurrection, though not yet written down, can be dated to within two years of that very event."* [33] An oral testimony would fit well with Strobel's statement. Such oral traditions increased, and Creeds, such as the Nicene Creed, were developed. This was created at the Council of Nicaea in 325 A.D.[34] Some people today can recite the Nicene Creed without looking at the text. Early Christians probably could do the same with the oral testimony.

How Long After an Event can a Historian Accurately Write About it?

This is an important question, and I have seen various answers. One said, '1 to 2 generations after the event', another said, '50 to 75 years', and another said that exaggerations start occurring about 100 years after an event. The longer the time between the event and its retelling, the more likely it is that exaggerations and falsehoods can creep in. Retellings can become so

[33] Strobel, L. 1998. The Case for Christ. Zondervan, Grand Rapids, MI.
[34] https://en.wikipedia.org/wiki/Nicene_Creed

exaggerated that the story is distorted and becomes a myth.

The New Testament writings pass this test because so many were written less than one generation after the event.

How Does this Time Lag Compare with Other Famous People?

Two 'early' biographies of Alexander the Great (336-323 B.C.) were written by Arrian (86-160 A.D.) and Plutarch (46-199 A.D.) over 300 years after his death. As stated above, such late reporting of events can result in false statements creeping in.

We have evidence of Alexander's existence from his conquered territories, the cities named after him, and his generals such as Ptolemy and Seluceus. Both played significant roles in the Middle East. Nevertheless, 300 years is a long time. The evidence for a historical Jesus is much closer to when he lived than for Alexander. If you believe Alexander the Great was a living, breathing person, you should do the same for Jesus Christ.

PART 1: ANALYSIS

I used to do experiments in soybean fields where different treatments (such as reduced tillage) were randomly assigned in a block. A block was a rectangular section of a soybean field. There were always at least four blocks; this is a randomized complete block design. The blocks were replicates. Scientists value randomization and replication because they help produce valid data. We cannot do this with historical data; instead, we piece together a summary based on all the local data.

History occurs once and isn't repeated; historical data are observational data. For example, there are people alive today who saw the Kennedy assassination or the Twin Towers on 9-11. Their testimony varies due to their location and role. A firefighter on the ground on 9-11 had a different view than a government worker in a nearby building. Both saw the event but would report differing details.

SUMMARY

1. The New Testament has been transmitted from disciple to student, and those men all describe the crucifixion and resurrection of Jesus.
2. Outside data sources, such as Josephus and Eusebius, affirm Jesus' death and resurrection and concur with Polycarp and Irenaeus.
3. Another confirmation comes from the scribes' precise methods of creating copies of ancient documents. In the scientific world, this is an extremely careful and exact handling of data. Further, the data were verified by other people (i.e., Rabbis). This care is impressive.
4. The Codex Sinaiticus, dating from 300 to 399 A.D., is amazingly close to the King James Version, dating from 1611 A.D. It is a telling example of how the New Testament has been handed down from generation to generation.
5. There are thousands of ancient copies of the New Testament and their uniformity strengthens the hypothesis that it has been accurately handed down to us.
6. The New Testament was written soon enough after Jesus' death that false information is unlikely.
7. What we see today is what was originally written.

PART 2: ARCHEOLOGICAL AND SUPPORTING DATA

I respect archeologists who dedicate their lives to understanding the past. Much of their work is spent studying moveable remains, such as documents and small artifacts; and immoveable remains, such as ancient buildings and large statues. They also investigate human remains. Archeologists cannot conduct experiments and replicate their work. However, they can use scientific means to carbon date their findings and determine the chemical composition of an artifact. For example, the type and style of paint used on an ancient pottery shard can tell us when and where somebody made it.

Is There Archeological Evidence for People and Places Mentioned in the New Testament?

Archeological discoveries can confirm or alter historical views. There should be archeological discoveries confirming the New Testament if it depicts real people and events.

Archeologists can only discover what has survived the more than 1,900 years since Jesus' death. Jesus had no home so that archeologists won't find it: *"And Jesus said to him, 'Foxes have holes and birds of the air have nests, but the Son of Man has no place to lay His head.'"* Matthew 8:20. However, we <u>can</u> read about archeological evidence for well-known people and places at the time of Jesus.

There have been many archeological discoveries related to the New Testament! There are so many that several books describe the wealth of archeological evidence. For example, the Zondervan Handbook of Biblical Archeology has over 100 pages devoted to archeological discoveries specific to the New Testament.[35] The Associates for Biblical Research have a YouTube channel that includes shows such as, 'Jesus Christ-The Top Ten Archaeological Discoveries'[36] and 'The Apostle Paul, the Top 10 Archeological Discoveries.'[37] I list below several important New Testament archeological discoveries.

CAIAPHAS' OSSUARY: Extra-biblical sources verify that Joseph Caiaphas was a historical person who was a chief priest in Jerusalem from 18 to 37 A.D. Caiaphas was the High Priest when Jesus was tried and crucified. The High Priest was a liaison between

---

[35] House, J. and H. House. 2017. Zondervan Handbook of Biblical Archeology. Zondervan, Grand Rapids, MI. 408 pp.
[36] https://www.youtube.com/watch?v=Jt1ASX1Vi7w
[37] https://www.youtube.com/watch?v=-ucqHF_JVRw

the Roman authorities at the time and the Jewish people. However, the Roman authorities hand-picked the High Priests, so the Priests' allegiance to the Jews could be questionable. This position carried power, stature, and wealth- and all three were at least partially attached to the Roman authority. Caiaphas was the son-in-law of the earlier High Priest, Annas.

An ossuary (bone box) was discovered in 1990 in Jerusalem that had the remains of a 60-year-old man, a woman, two teenage boys, and two infants. Storing bones in a bone box was a customary practice in ancient Judea. The deceased Jews were wrapped in linen, and the body was placed in a burial crypt. Relatives entered the crypt after a year and put the bones in an ossuary, a clay box.

This wasn't just any ossuary, though. This one was ornate and was inscribed in Aramaic with, 'Yehosef bar Qafa,' which is a reference to Joseph Caiaphas.[38] According to the Zondervan Handbook of Biblical Archeology, *"… there is no other person in Israel, known as Caiaphas, who would satisfy the requirements for this*

FROM: Wikimedia Commons:
Ossuary_of_the_high_priest_
Joseph_Caiaphas_P1180839.JPG

---

[38] https://en.wikipedia.org/wiki/Caiaphas_ossuary

ossuary." The High Priest Caiaphas was a real person, and his remains exist.

HEROD THE GREAT'S FORTRESS: Matthew recounts this story: *"After Jesus was born in Bethlehem in Judea, during the time of King Herod, Magi from the east came to Jerusalem and asked, 'Where is the one who has been born king of the Jews? We saw his star when it rose and have come to worship him.' When King Herod heard this he was disturbed, and all Jerusalem with him. When he had called together all the people's chief priests and teachers of the law, he asked them where the Messiah was to be born."* Matthew 2:1-4. Herod is a known historical figure, and his fortress at Kypros was discovered near Jericho.[39] Archeologists found alabaster tubs there, which were made from local stone. Herod had other palaces, too. Archeologists also found Herod's 8-foot-long stone sarcophagus in 2007 in Herodium, near Bethlehem.[40] Herod died in Jericho in 4 B.C.

PONTIUS PILATE INSCRIPTION: Pontius Pilate was also an actual person, not a myth. He was the governor of Judea and Jesus was taken to him. *"Early in the morning, all the chief priests and the elders of the people made their plans how to have Jesus executed.*

[39] https://biblearchaeology.org/current-events-list/4910-herod-the-greats-alabaster-tubs-made-with-stone-from-israel-not-egypt
[40] https://www.historyhit.com/the-discovery-of-king-herods-tomb/

So they bound him, led him away and handed him over to Pilate the governor." Matthew 27:1-3.

The Pontius Pilate inscription was discovered in 1961 on a piece of ancient carved limestone. The text is to Emperor Tiberius from Pontius Pilate.[41] The inscription was written in Latin and translates as, *"Pontius Pilate, prefect of Judea, dedicated a temple to the people of Caesarea in honor of Tiberius."* This significant find verifies that Pontius Pilate was a real person who was the Prefect (Roman governor) of Judea at the time of Jesus. Caesarea Philippi, known as Banias in later times, was inhabited for 2,000 years until 1967 when it was abandoned.

Sometime later, Pontius Pilate was ordered to Rome to stand trial for cruelty after his attack on the Samaritans. He may have been exonerated and lived out his life in Italy, even perhaps as a Christian.[42]

OSSUARY OF JAMES, JESUS' BROTHER: This is a 20-inch-long limestone bone box with the inscription, *"James, son of Joseph, brother of Jesus"* in Aramaic.[43] It was so controversial in the past that the Israel Antiquities Authority held a trial charging the owner

[41] https://en.wikipedia.org/wiki/Pilate_stone
[42] Kennedy, T. 2022. Excavating the Evidence for Jesus: The Archeology and History of Christ and the Gospels. Harvest House Publishing, Eugene, OR. 299 pp.
[43] https://www.biblicalarchaeology.org/daily/biblical-artifacts/artifacts-and-the-bible/is-the-brother-of-jesus-inscription-on-the-james-ossuary-a-forgery/

with forgery and other crimes. He was found not guilty. Recent evidence, though, shows that the ossuary is genuine. The phrase about James has a patina that shows that the entire phrase was written on the ossuary before it was placed in a tomb in Jerusalem. The ossuary dates to when James would have died and was made from local Jerusalem limestone. The craftsmanship and style of the ossuary match those of 1st century A.D. Jerusalem.[44] There is no known other James, who was the son of Joseph and had a brother named Jesus from this period. Finally, a statistical study of those three names showed that there were <u>fewer than</u> two James with a father named Joseph and a brother named Jesus at this time. Most scholars now believe that this is the ossuary of Jesus' brother James. It is the earliest known archeological evidence of Jesus and his brother James.

POOL OF SILOAM: Jesus healed a blind man and told the man to wash in the Pool of Siloam, *"'As long as I am in the world, I am the light of the world.' Having said these things, he spit on the ground and made mud with the saliva. Then he anointed the man's eyes with the mud and said to him, 'Go, wash in the pool of Siloam'...So he went and washed and came back seeing."* John 9:5-6 ESV. The remains of the Pool of Siloam were discovered in the City of David in

---

[44] Kennedy, T. 2022. Excavating the Evidence for Jesus: The Archeology and History of Christ and the Gospels. Harvest House Publishing, Eugene, OR. 299 pp.

Jerusalem in 2004. The pool was 225 feet long and in the shape of a trapezoid.[45] It is a sacred site.

THE APOSTLE PETER'S HOUSE: Archeologists discovered an ancient stone home in Capernaum, where Peter and several Apostles lived when they met Jesus. The stone house is 483 square feet.

FROM: Wikimedia Commons: The_ House_of_Peter_(25258320084).jpg

An open courtyard surrounded it, and it had a thatched roof. [46] A fishhook was found on the floor inside. This modest home was discovered under a Byzantine-era church. Many believe this is Peter's house because the church was built over it.

YEHOHANAN INSCRIPTION: Yehohanan was a man who was crucified in the 1st century A.D. so he might have been a contemporary of Jesus.[47] Crucifixion was a common way for Rome to execute prisoners, but this is the only example known of someone crucified at the time of Jesus. A heel bone with a nail driven through

---

[45] https://www.biblicalarchaeology.org/daily/
biblical-sites-places/biblical-archaeology-sites/
the-siloam-pool-where-jesus-healed-the-blind-man/
[46] https://www.biblicalarchaeology.org/daily/
biblical-sites-places/biblical-archaeology-sites/
the-house-of-peter-the-home-of-jesus-in-capernaum/
[47] https://www.timesofisrael.com/
in-a-stone-box-a-rare-trace-of-crucifixion/

it was found in this man's ossuary (see photo). The nail was not driven through the top of the foot but through the side, showing that a nail was used to affix each foot to the cross. Archeologists also found wood remnants on the nail, showing that the nail had a wooden washer to help prevent it from tearing out.[48]

JESUS'S TOMB: An edicule ("little house") surrounds the remains of the possible tomb of Jesus in the Church of the Holy Sepulchre in Jerusalem.[49] This is the holiest site in the Christian world, commemorating the traditional location of Jesus' tomb.

Representation of spike in ankle of Yehohanan.

FROM: Zev Radovan/ Alamy Stock Photo

JACOB'S WELL: Jesus met with a Samaritan woman at Jacob's well, *"And he had to pass through Samaria. So he came to a town of Samaria called Sychar, near the field that Jacob had given to his son Joseph. Jacob's well was there; so Jesus, wearied as he was from his journey, was sitting beside the well. It was about the sixth hour."* John 4:4-6. Jacob's Well is at the foot of Mount

[48] https://www.youtube.com/watch?v=V0gNIL5GAdE
[49] https://www.biblicalarchaeology.org/daily/biblical-sites-places/jerusalem/inside-the-church-of-the-holy-sepulchre/

Gerizim, south of Askar in modern-day Bahrain.[50] Christian, Jewish, and Muslim faiths accept this site as Jacob's Well.

NAZARETH INSCRIPTION: This is a 1st-century stone tablet from Caesar discovered in Nazareth and appears to date to the reign of Roman Emperor Claudius (41 to 54 A.D.). *"It imposes a death penalty in Israel for anyone caught moving bodies from family tombs, and specifically 'sepulcher-sealing tombs,' such as the one Jesus was buried in."[51]*

FROM: Wikimedia Commons: Nazareth_Inscription.jpg

Grave robbing has been an issue since ancient times, but the robbers usually steal booty rather than bodies. This mandate may be in response to the resurrection of Jesus. The Pharisees and Sadducees bribed the guards so that they'd say that the body was stolen when anyone asked them. (Matthew 28:11-15).

You've seen ten archeological discoveries, and they all confirm the historical data. Zondervan's 2017 Handbook of Biblical Archeology lists 37 archeological

---

[50] https://biblearchaeologyreport.com/2021/04/02/top-ten-discoveries-related-to-jesus/

[51] https://biblearchaeologyreport.com/2021/04/02/top-ten-discoveries-related-to-jesus/

discoveries about the New Testament. Ancient cities mentioned in the New Testament have been found such as Bethlehem, Capernaum, Caesarea Philippi, Ephesus, Laodicea, and Smyrna. Archeologists confirmed that the Pool of Siloam and Jacob's Well have been found. Archeologists discovered the Temple of Artemis and the Theatre of Ephesus. They also may have found Apostle Peter's stone house. Cities, temples, pools, and wells were made of stone and survived for us to find.

Archeological evidence about people is more difficult to find. Even so, Caiaphas, Pontius Pilate, and James, Jesus's brother, have artifacts. Roman Emperors Augustus, Tiberius, Claudius, and Nero are well-known historical figures with a wealth of archeological data supporting their existence. It is also possible that the house of Mary and Joseph, Jesus' parents, has been found. A house in Nazareth was revered during the Byzantine Period as the childhood home of Jesus and a church was built next to it.[52]

No archeological discoveries contradict the New Testament narrative. This is also an important finding. The archeological data affirm the historical data.

---

[52] Kennedy, T. 2022. Excavating the Evidence for Jesus: The Archeology and History of Christ and the Gospels. Harvest House Publishing, Eugene, OR. 299 pp.

Do Corroborating Data Exist for the New Testament Narrative?

CULTURE OF THE TIMES

Understanding the culture of ancient Judea at the time of Jesus' birth is essential. The human lifespan was about 35 years, with high infant mortality. Diseases were common in the area, including malaria, smallpox, plague, tuberculosis, and skin diseases such as leprosy. Many of these diseases are still with us. For example, I traveled to Mali in the early 1990s and walked by a beggar with leprosy in Bamako, the capital.

Jerusalem was a small city with an estimated population of about 75,000, and most industries in it were craft-based.[53] There were wool- and leather-makers, builders, olive oil producers, and high-end luxury goods makers. The small town of Nazareth was about 200 to 400 people, so it was a hamlet. Most houses were built with stone and had little wood (mostly rafters, beds, utensils, etc.).

A Jewish woman was to marry and have children, especially male children. Motherhood was highly honored! Interestingly, the woman was the religious instructor in the house. She would also perform

---

[53] https://christianfaithguide.com/how-big-was-jerusalem-during-jesus-time-jerusalems-size-during-the-time-of-jesus/

charitable work and care for the poor. Women also sold goods that they made, such as clothing.

A Jewish man was the head of the household and was the only legal representative of the house. He had to learn a craft (e.g., carpenter) and make a profit. He protected the property, the family, and the domesticated animals on it. He was also occasionally called to be a soldier.

Jewish laws at the time gave women few rights. We see this in the Book of Ruth, where Boaz had to redeem Ruth so that she didn't have to glean fields for food after the pickers finished each day. Agreements were made between men and not women. This was a patriarchal society.

THE NEW TESTAMENT FEATURES WOMEN

The New Testament continues the theme in the Old Testament of women having prominent roles, such as Rebekah (Genesis 27), Tamar (Genesis 38), Rahab (Joshua 2), Jezebel (1 Kings 19), and Bathsheba (2 Samuel 11). Several women are mentioned at the crucifixion: *"Some women were watching from a distance. Among them were Mary Magdalene, Mary the mother of James the younger and of Joseph, and Salome. In Galilee these women had followed him and cared for his needs. Many other women who had come up with him to Jerusalem were also there."* Mark 15:40-41. Only one Apostle is mentioned- John.

Mary Magdalene is the first one at the empty tomb: *"Now Mary stood outside the tomb crying. As she wept, she bent over to look into the tomb and saw two angels in white, seated where Jesus' body had been, one at the head and the other at the foot. They asked her, 'Woman, why are you crying?' 'They have taken my Lord away,' she said, 'and I don't know where they have put him.' At this, she turned around and saw Jesus standing there, but she did not realize that it was Jesus. He asked her, 'Woman, why are you crying? Who is it you are looking for?' Thinking he was the gardener, she said, 'Sir, if you have carried him away, tell me where you have put him, and I will get him.' Jesus said to her, 'Mary.' She turned toward him and cried out in Aramaic, 'Rabboni!' (which means 'Teacher')."* John 20:11-16.

The New Testament also describes Jesus interacting with a woman at a well (John 4:4-26), Jesus talking to Martha and Mary (but not men) at the resurrection of Lazarus (John 11), and Jesus being anointed with expensive perfume by a woman (Matthew 26:6-11).

If this were fiction, why would someone write something counter to its male-dominated society? It would have been more credible to people at the time to have men as the eyewitnesses to Jesus' crucifixion and men

STATISTICALLY SIGNIFICANT, By Tim Mack

as the first two people that Jesus talked to at the resurrection of Lazarus.

The other thing that strikes readers of the New Testament is how people are flawed. Peter denies Jesus three times (Matthew 26:69-75). Do you think Peter would write or allow others to write this if it were false? What a thing to write... 'Gee, I deny God's son.' Jesus also tells Peter, *"Get behind me, Satan!"* (Matthew 16:23). Why add that to a fictional account? It makes your fictional character seem quite flawed. Given the patriarchal society at the time, it seems out of character to create so many flawed characters in a narrative. If you are writing the truth, however, this makes sense.

The Apostle John also had a 'D'oh!' moment. Jesus, John, and James were on their way to Samaria. We read, *"As the time approached for him to be taken up to heaven, Jesus resolutely set out for Jerusalem. And he sent messengers on ahead, who went into a Samaritan village to get things ready for him; but the people there did not welcome him, because he was heading for Jerusalem. When the disciples James and John saw this, they asked, 'Lord, do you want us to call fire down from heaven to destroy them?'"* Luke 9:51-54. James and John wanted to destroy the Samaritans who weren't welcoming Jesus. Sometime later, we read in Acts 8:14, *"When the apostles in Jerusalem heard that Samaria had accepted the word of God, they sent Peter and John to Samaria."*

These are the people that John wanted to burn with fire from Heaven! What did John feel when he saw the Samaritans accept the Gospel? In Mark 3:17, Jesus nicknamed John and his brother James as Boanerges…Sons of Thunder. Perhaps it was because they thundered statements such as, *"…call fire down from heaven to destroy them…"*

These statements strongly suggest that they are authentic recordings of events because fallible people make mistakes, and the Bible depicts people as flawed human beings…which we are.

There is also the persecution of Christians described in the New Testament, such as the stoning to death of Steven (Acts 7:54-60). If this were all a myth, then why would the Christians be persecuted? There are enough of these incidents in the New Testament to show that this is the truth.

DATA FROM OUTSIDE OF
THE NEW TESTAMENT

There are sources - ancient historians- who mentioned Jesus. Here are three such instances:

TACITUS: He is a Roman historian and senator who lived from 56-120 A.D. The Roman Empire at this time was a pagan, polytheistic empire. Therefore, we might think of Tacitus as someone who isn't going to believe in one God. Tacitus wrote, *"Consequently, to get rid of the report, Nero fastened the guilt and inflicted the most exquisite tortures on a class hated for their abominations, called Christians by the populace. Christus, from whom the name had its origin, suffered the extreme penalty during the reign of Tiberius at the hands of one of our procurators, Pontius Pilatus..."*[54] Tacitus' account states that Jesus died at the hands of Pontius Pilate.

PLINY THE YOUNGER: The full name of this scholar was Gaius Plinius Caecilius Secundus, and he was the Governor of Bithynia in 110 A.D. Pliny interrogated Christians and thought little of them. He wrote, *"Meanwhile, in the case of those who were denounced to me as Christians, I have observed the following procedure: I interrogated these as to whether they were Christians; those who confessed I interrogated a second and a third time, threatening them with punishment; those who persisted I ordered executed...They asserted, however, that the sum and substance of their fault or error had been that they were accustomed to meet on a fixed day before dawn and sing responsively a hymn to Christ as to a god..."*[55] Pliny isn't a fan of Christians!

---

[54] The Annals of Tacitus, Book 15. https://en.wikisource.org/wiki/The_Annals_(Tacitus)/Book_15#44
[55] https://faculty.georgetown.edu/jod/texts/pliny.html

JOSEPHUS: This Jewish historian wrote about Jesus' death, and I quoted Josephus in the Important Historians section of this book.

PART 2: ANALYSIS

We have archeological analyses of physical data, which is good. Others can visit, examine, and evaluate these data. For example, other archeologists can visit Laodicea and either confirm or deny that the site is that city. The archeological data affirm the historical information in the New Testament, and none contradict it.

The New Testament narrative unusually depicts women in prominent ways, countering what a fictional account would say. A patriarchal society at the time would not have supported such a 'counterculture' narrative.

Three ancient authors discussed Jesus: one Jewish historian, one Roman historian, and one Roman senator. Josephus wrote about Jesus Christ himself. Tacitus rather tellingly describes Jesus' death, and Pliny discusses the interrogation of Christians. Other historians and theologians have examined these ancient documents over hundreds of years, and the documents have withstood the test of time. Yes, the internal and external data reinforce the New Testament narrative.

Summary

1. Many ancient cities, temples, and other stone structures have been found, verifying locations in the New Testament.

2. Archeological findings confirm the existence of Caiaphas, Pontius Pilate, James the brother of Jesus, and four Roman Emperors mentioned in the New Testament.

3. All the archeological discoveries related to the New Testament confirm the biblical text and none contradict it.

4. The archeological evidence continues to grow as archeologists make new discoveries.

5. The 'counterculture' narrative featuring women in the New Testament is unlikely to be fictional. Further, people's flaws in the New Testament are a sign of authenticity.

6. Writings from outside sources reinforce the New Testament narrative.

PART 3: MEDICAL, GEOLOGICAL, AND ASTRONOMICAL DATA

Did Jesus Actually Die?

This is one of the most critical questions that we must answer. After all, Jesus cannot be resurrected from the dead if he didn't die! The resurrection of Jesus is the founding stone of Christian belief. If Jesus never died but just was wounded, then Christianity is based on false assumptions. Paul summarizes the issues well in his letter to the believers in Corinth: *"But if it is preached that Christ has been raised from the dead, how can some of you say that there is no resurrection of the dead? If there is no resurrection of the dead, then not even Christ has been raised. And if Christ has not been raised, our preaching is useless and so is your faith… And if Christ has not been raised, your faith is futile; you are still in your sins. Then those also who have fallen asleep in Christ are lost. If only for this life we have hope in Christ, we are of all people most to be pitied."* 1 Corinthians 15:12-19.

Describing how someone dies is gruesome. The descriptions may be too intense for young readers.

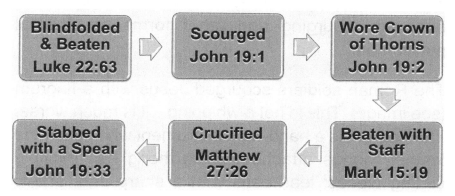

| Blindfolded & Beaten Luke 22:63 | ⇨ | Scourged John 19:1 | ⇨ | Wore Crown of Thorns John 19:2 |

| Stabbed with a Spear John 19:33 | ⇦ | Crucified Matthew 27:26 | ⇦ | Beaten with Staff Mark 15:19 |

Above is an overview of what happened to Jesus.

PUNCHING AND SCOURGING

"The men who were guarding Jesus began mocking and beating him." Luke 22:63. Jesus was probably beaten more than once and this is the first beating.[56] These were professional soldiers of a Roman garrison and were trained

FROM: Wikimedia Commons: Flagrum.jpg

---

[56] https://religiousaffections.org/articles/articles-on-theology/the-two-beatings-of-jesus/

to fight, of course. They knew how to punch without hurting their hands and where to punch to damage someone.

"Then Pilate therefore took Jesus, and scourged him." John 19:1 KJV. Some translations use 'flogged' while others use 'whipped.' There is a significant difference between scourging and other forms of physical punishment.

The Roman soldiers scourged Jesus with a flagrum (see image). This is not a whipping...it is much worse. The flagrum is a hand-held instrument with up to nine leather thongs attached. Each thong has multiple cutting pieces: lead balls with a sharp end, sheep bone shards, wire pieces, sharp stones, etc. A flagrum with nine thongs and three cutting pieces would create 27 cuts and gouges with a single strike. The Roman unit that tortured prisoners was experienced at using the flagrum because there were many scourgings. There was even a position in the Roman army called a 'Quaestionarius.' This person knew how to interrogate (i.e., torture) prisoners physically.

The prisoner would be naked and chained to a scourging pillar, which was in a relatively permanent location. Prisoners were struck from the shoulders to the knees with the flagrum. The soldier didn't strike the prisoner's neck because the flagrum could tear the aorta and the prisoner would very rapidly die. In the Old

Testament, prisoners could be struck up to 39 times. Typically, a Rabbi would be there to prevent a Jewish prisoner from being struck more than 39 times, but the New Testament lists no such Rabbi. On the contrary, the Pharisees and Sadducees wanted Jesus to die: *"Then one of them, named Caiaphas, who was high priest that year, spoke up, 'You know nothing at all! You do not realize that it is better for you that one man die for the people than that the whole nation perish.'... So from that day on they plotted to take his life."* John 11:49-53. Jesus was a threat to their authority, their way of life, their status, and their wealth.[57]

It is therefore unlikely that any Rabbi was there to stop the scourging of Jesus at 39 strikes. Also, the local Roman garrisons distant from Rome usually recruited soldiers from surrounding areas. The Romans wouldn't have gotten soldiers from the Jews, who objected to Roman occupation. The Samaritans were nearby, and Samaritans detested Jews. Samaria was a province that was originally part of the northern Kingdom of Israel, and their religious beliefs differed from the Jews. There were even occasional border skirmishes between the two provinces. One can only guess how cruelly Samaritan soldiers would treat someone touted as the 'King of the Jews.'

Flagrum strikes inflict horrific damage to the human body. I've read that the soldier using the flagrum would

---

[57] https://www.blueletterbible.org/faq/don_stewart/don_stewart_248.cfm

strike one side of the prisoner so the thongs would wrap around the chest and then pull back hard so that the cutting pieces ripped through the prisoner's flesh, tearing skin, nerves, blood vessels, and muscle. It could expose the lungs and intestines. This damage could be fatal in ancient times due to massive blood loss and infection. Also, *"The victim would periodically vomit, experience tremors and seizures, and have bouts of fainting."*[58]

The flagrum mutilated the prisoner's back and broke ribs. Liver damage was possible. Some people did recover from scourging. I've read that a few could no longer lift their arms over their heads. This form of punishment is so heinous that no country uses it today.

Let's assume that a flagrum with just five leather thongs was used and that each thong had three cutting pieces. If Jesus had been scourged 40 times with this instrument, then he would have had 40 times (5 times 3) wounds, which is 600 wounds! A massive amount of blood loss would occur from that many wounds.

Roman scourgings also had one lesser-known feature. Archeologists have found small stone pillars with a shallow depression in the top for salt at some scourging sites. Salt was at least sometimes thrown

---

[58] https://catholicinsight.com/
the-physical-effects-of-the-scourging- and-crucifixion-of-jesus/

onto the prisoner's body after scourging. The Romans may have copied the Carthaginians in this because the Carthaginians used vinegar, salt, and even fire to worsen the prisoner's pain.[59] Imagine the pain Jesus would have felt if salt had been thrown onto his wounds. To me, this is brutal and inhuman.

CROWN OF THORNS

"The soldiers twisted together a crown of thorns and put it on his head." John 19:2. No one knows what plant the Romans used to make the crown of thorns. It might have been Ziziphus spina-christi, the Christ's thorn jujube. This small and spiny evergreen tree commonly grew in the area, making it easy to find. The Bible verse says that the soldiers twisted together a crown, so it was composed of several flexible branches. If it was the Christ's thorn jujube tree, then the thorns were about an inch long. Other candidate plants could have had spines of up to two inches long.

The human head has a tremendous number of arteries and veins. In 'The Crucifixion, a Medical Perspective,' a modern trauma surgeon examined the account of Jesus's crown of thorns and noted that it would have caused excessive blood loss.[60] He has had patients

---

[59] https://medium.com/flamma-saga/the-cross-and-the-crucified-a-history-and-culture-of-crucifixion-c6b1406ca105
[60] https://www.youtube.com/watch?v=T-EVfxABSoU&list=PL4-Ug0qqm9edrVG0zaMtUoajh175cekFi&index=108

die from excessive blood loss from a head wound. The long thorns digging deeply into Jesus' scalp certainly would have added to the great blood loss that Jesus had from the scourging.

BEATEN WITH A STAFF OR REED

"Again and again they struck him on the head with a staff and spit on him. Falling on their knees, they paid homage to him. And when they had mocked him, they took off the purple robe and put his own clothes on him." Mark 15:19-20. Several translations of this verse use 'reed' instead of staff. Reeds typically grew in or near water and would have been dried for use as a staff. A common reed in ancient Israel was Phragmites australis, which grew to 20 feet tall. Being beaten on the head with a stick or reed by professional soldiers would be damaging and probably disfiguring. Spitting on Jesus would be in character for Samaritan soldiers who detested Jews.

JESUS IS CRUCIFIED-
CARRYING THE CROSS

"At its height, Rome crucified up to 500 Jews per day."[61] Crucifixion became a daily event. It seems likely that there was a standard location for crucifying Roman

---

[61] https://www.crucifixio.com/crucifixion/roman

prisoners, and the Bible's reference to Golgotha may be such a place: *"They came to a place called Golgotha (which means "the place of the skull") ... When they had crucified him, they divided up his clothes by casting lots... Above his head they placed the written charge against him: THIS IS JESUS, THE KING OF THE JEWS. Two rebels were crucified with him, one on his right and one on his left."* Matthew 27:33-38.

Crucifixion involves a wooden cross. In ancient times, Rome used palm, oak, pine, cypress, and cedar for crosses. Crosses were heavy! The estimated weight of a cross was over 300 lbs.[62] Most prisoners didn't carry the 300 lb. cross; instead, the prisoners carried the cross piece, known as the Patibulum. This would have weighed about 70-150 lbs. The beatings, scourging, crown of thorns, and being battered with a staff severely weakened Jesus. The blood loss alone would have made him out of breath. Trying to carry a heavy load in that condition would have been impossible.

Simon of Cyrene helped: *"A certain man from Cyrene, Simon, the father of Alexander and Rufus, was passing by on his way in from the country, and they forced him to carry the cross."* Mark 15:21. Cyrene was a real city of about 5,000 people at the time, in what is now modern-day Libya.

---

[62] https://www.biblword.net/
what-is-the-weight-of-the-cross-that-jesus-carried/

JESUS IS CRUCIFIED- NAILED TO THE CROSS

The New Testament says that Jesus' hands and feet were nailed to the cross. Roman crucifixion varied and some prisoners had their arms tied to the crosspiece rather than being nailed to it.[63] Nevertheless, we know that Jesus was nailed to the cross. There is no ancient Greek word for 'wrist' in the New Testament, so 'hand' refers to both the hand and the wrist. We don't know if the soldiers drove the nails into the hands or the wrists.[64] As we saw earlier, the soldiers may have used wooden washers with iron nails to prevent them from tearing through the prisoner's hands. The median nerve could have been damaged depending on where the 7-to-9-inch nails entered the hand or wrist. Damaging that nerve is excruciating!

Jesus was most likely crucified naked.[65] This would have been the most humiliating form of execution for a Jew. Jesus had to lie down to be nailed to the Patibulum cross piece. That would have been painful as his crown of thorns was pushed into his head by the ground and his raw & bleeding back would have rubbed on the ground. More bleeding would have occurred.

---

[63] https://www.biblicalarchaeology.org/daily/biblical-topics/crucifixion/roman-crucifixion-methods-reveal-the-history-of-crucifixion/
[64] https://www.gotquestions.org/nails-hands-wrists.html
[65] https://christianity.stackexchange.com/questions/37196/was-jesus-crucified-naked

Roman soldiers would have picked up the Patibulum, with Jesus attached, and affixed it to the vertical post.[66] Jesus' weight would have been on the nails in his hands or wrists. Then, soldiers nailed Jesus' feet to the vertical posts. Dislocating an arm from the shoulder seems common as this lifting occurs. Jim Caviezel portrayed Jesus in the movie, 'The Passion of the Christ,' and he had a shoulder separation during the filming of the crucifixion.[67]

Breathing isn't easy on a cross. The standard process is for your diaphragm to move down to enlarge the lungs as you inhale, and your diaphragm moves up to compress the lungs as you exhale. The weight of Jesus' body on the cross caused the diaphragm to move down, making it harder to exhale. Jesus, like other crucified prisoners, pushed up with his legs to be able to exhale effectively. This up-and-down motion caused terrible pain in his feet with nails in them and tired his legs. Someone could still breathe without doing this but he'd get less oxygen.[68] Remember that Jesus still had the crown of thorns and wounds all over his body, so pushing up with his legs caused his head and back to rub up against the cross. He bled even more.

---

[66] https://www.apu.edu/articles/the-science-of-the-crucifixion/
[67] https://www.imdb.com/title/tt0335345/trivia/
[68] https://www.ncregister.com/blog/13-myths-of-the-crucifixion

HYPOVOLEMIC SHOCK AND JESUS

"…Jesus said, *"I am thirsty."* John 19:28. He had lost a massive amount of blood from his beatings, the crown of thorns, and the scourging. This loss of blood caused Jesus' thirst. Medically speaking, Jesus was in hypovolemic shock.

'Hypo' means low, and 'volemic' means volume, so this is where there isn't enough blood to carry oxygen to the body effectively. Hypovolemic shock is a severe medical condition that requires immediate attention because of the danger of organ failure. Your pulse rate increases to compensate for the reduced blood volume,[69] and this higher pulse can eventually lead to cardiac arrest. You also breathe faster, which we've already seen is hard for someone on a cross to do. Modern therapy would involve oxygen and a blood transfusion, but Jesus couldn't do that. There are stages to hypovolemic shock. In an early stage, the body redirects blood away from the limbs and sends it to the heart and other organs. In the next stage, your blood pressure drops dangerously low.

The decreased oxygen from the now lower blood pressure would have caused plasma (i.e., watery fluid) to leak from Jesus' blood vessels into the tissue. This plus the trauma of a scourging and crucifixion, could

---

[69] https://www.webmd.com/a-to-z-guides/hypovolemic-shock

cause <u>pericardial and/or pulmonary effusions</u>.[70] The heart and the lungs have membranous sacs around them that normally hold fluid. In an effusion, excessive amounts of fluid accumulate (see image). An effusion can be dangerous and may lead to heart failure. Jesus was dying. The loss of blood and extreme trauma was too much for his body.

PERICARDIAL EFFUSION

Normal Heart   Abnormal Heart

Sac around heart is enlarged and filled with fluid

ADAPTED FROM: Wikimedia Commons: Pericarditis_can_progress_to_pericardial_effusion_and_eventually_cardiac_tamponade.jpg

THE DEATH OF JESUS

"A jar of wine vinegar was there, so they soaked a sponge in it, put the sponge on a stalk of the hyssop plant, and lifted it to Jesus' lips. When he had received the drink, Jesus said, 'It is finished.' With that, he bowed his head and gave up his spirit." John 19:28-30. The Roman soldiers broke the legs of two criminals crucified next to Jesus but didn't do this to Jesus: *"The soldiers therefore came and broke the legs of the first man who had been crucified with Jesus, and then those of the other. But when they came to Jesus and found that he was already dead, they did not break*

---

[70] https://my.clevelandclinic.org/health/diseases/17351-pericardial-effusion#symptoms-and-causes

his legs." John 19:32-33. Breaking the legs makes it so hard to breathe that most people would suffocate.

A Roman soldier stabbed Jesus with a spear to ensure that he was dead: *"...one of the soldiers pierced Jesus' side with a spear, bringing a sudden flow of blood and water. The man who saw it has given testimony, and his testimony is true. He knows that he tells the truth, and he testifies so that you also may believe."* John 19:34-35.

I looked at 27 versions of this verse, and none say which side the Roman soldier was standing on when he stabbed Jesus. Roman soldiers knew where to thrust a sword or spear to kill someone. Their knowledge of human anatomy was good enough to know where to thrust to stab someone in the heart. Therefore, the Roman soldier probably pierced Jesus' heart after death.

The *"...a sudden flow of blood and water"* that the Apostle John mentions is a medically correct description of someone who has been stabbed in the heart or lung. The 'water' would have been the clear fluid in the pericardial or pulmonary sac. John made a point about his testimony being accurate and true. Why? Well, priests downplayed this detail for years because they couldn't believe that a human could 'bleed water!' This medically correct description adds authenticity to this first-person account from John.

The Roman soldiers were responsible for ensuring that all three crucified prisoners were dead. That was their job. The Roman army had brutal discipline for soldiers who didn't do their job correctly. For example, falling asleep on guard duty was punishable by death.[71] Other corporal punishments included being beaten or having their clothes set on fire. The soldiers would have broken his legs if there was any possibility that Jesus was alive. They didn't. There wasn't anyone there who cried out, *"He's still alive!"* The Jewish rabbis in attendance wanted him to die. They would have said something if Jesus was still alive. After all, they wanted to guarantee that he died.

I don't know how anyone could have survived being beaten, scourged, had a crown of thorns forced onto one's head, crucified, and then stabbed in either the lungs or the heart (my guess) with a spear. The scourging alone would have been deadly.

Jesus' dead body remained on the cross for a short while. Still, it would have been long enough for blood to accumulate in his lower extremities and for his body to cool. His lower extremities also would have turned bluish. Joseph of Arimathea and Nicodemus retrieved the body and would have noticed at once if Jesus weren't dead. His body would have been warm and his extremities would not have been distended

---

[71] https://neutralhistory.com/
discipline-in-the-roman-army-a-system-of-punishment-reward/

and bluish. Joseph and Nicodemus didn't notice that, though, because they would have stopped preparing his body for burial if they did.

SOURCES OUTSIDE THE BIBLE THAT CONFIRM JESUS' DEATH

John Ankerberg is an American Christian TV host and an ordained Baptist minister. He produced a video for his show entitled, 'Did Jesus Actually Die on the Cross?' and in this video, Professor Gary Habermas said there are 12 ancient authors from outside the Bible who affirm the death of Jesus.[72] One of those 12 is the Roman Historian Tacitus, who I previously quoted in the Archeology section of this book. Another is the Jewish Historian Josephus, who I mentioned in the Important Historians section of this book. Both discussed Jesus' crucifixion and death.

A third is Lucian, who was a Greek satirist. He was a pagan who had no reason to lie about Jesus. He wrote, *"The Christians. . . worship a man to this day – the distinguished personage who introduced this new cult, and was crucified on that account. . . . You see, these misguided creatures start with the general conviction that they are immortal for all time, which explains their contempt for death and self devotion . . . their lawgiver [taught] they are all brothers, from the*

---

[72] https://www.youtube.com/watch?v=zPWcoJ7oyl0

moment that they are converted, and deny the gods of Greece, and worship the crucified sage, and live after his laws. All this they take on faith..."[73] Lucian was mocking Christians. He also said that the 'sage' (Jesus) was crucified.

THE TEARING OF THE TEMPLE CURTAIN

Immediately after Jesus died, the colossal curtain or 'veil' tore: *"And when Jesus had cried out again in a loud voice, he gave up his spirit. At that moment the curtain of the temple was torn in two from top to bottom."* Matthew 27:50-51. We may read this today and think that it was an ordinary curtain.

What was the curtain made of? Genesis tells us: *"Make a curtain of blue, purple and scarlet yarn and finely twisted linen, with cherubim woven into it by a skilled worker. Hang it with gold hooks on four posts of acacia wood overlaid with gold and standing on four silver bases. Hang the curtain from the clasps and place the ark of the covenant law behind the curtain. The curtain will separate the Holy Place from the Most Holy Place."* Exodus 26:31-33.

In his work, 'The Life and Times of Jesus the Messiah,' Alfred Edersheim said that the curtain was 60 feet high and 30 feet wide[74]. What a large curtain!

---

[73] https://www.neverthirsty.org/about-christ/historical-quotes/lucian-of-samosata/

The Mishnah was written hundreds of years before Jesus was born and is the 1st significant collection of Jewish oral traditions. According to a translation of the Mishnah, *"Rabban Simeon b. Gamaliel says in the name of R. Simeon son of the Prefect: The veil was one handbreadth thick and was woven on [a loom having] seventy-two rods, and over each rod were twenty-four threads."*[74] A 'handbreadth thick' is about 3 to 4 inches, so this curtain was very thick. The curtain was so thick that the Blue Letter Bible says, *"Wild horses tied to each end of the veil, after it had been taken down, were not able to rend it asunder."*[75]

This curtain was torn from top to bottom. How could a curtain be torn that two horses could not tear? A person cutting such a long and thick curtain would have used a sword and would have hacked away for a long time, but it was torn and not cut. Further, the person would have started at the bottom and not 60 feet in the air. Without God's heavenly intervention, we cannot explain the tearing of this tall, thick, and strong curtain from the top down.

[74] https://cbumgardner.wordpress.com/2010/04/06/the-thickness-of-the-temple-veil/
[75] https://www.blueletterbible.org/Comm/mcgee_j_vernon/eBooks/tabernacle/chapter-viii-the-veil-which-was-rent.cfm

WAS THERE AN EARTHQUAKE?

An earthquake occurred when the curtain was torn: *"The earth shook, the rocks split and the tombs broke open."* Matthew 27:51-52. Earthquakes damage buildings and leave evidence for geologists to discover. Is there such evidence? Wikipedia has a list of earthquakes in the Middle East.[76] An earthquake that occurred between 26-36 A.D. is, ..."*identified in the geological strata of the Dead Sea and by Roman sources, which could be the same one reported by the Gospels to have taken place during the crucifixion of Jesus."* This statement references a refereed journal article by Williams.[77] The timing of this known earthquake <u>overlaps</u> Matthew's description of an earthquake.

WAS THERE AN ECLIPSE?

Some non-believers dismiss the darkness when Jesus died as, 'just a normal eclipse.' Was it? The ancient Jewish calendar was based on the sun and the moon. A year was composed of 12 months with 30 days in each month. This added up to 360 days so *"Keeping the lunar calendar coordinated with the seasons of the year required adding a 13th month to the lunar*

---

[76] https://en.wikipedia.org/wiki/List_of_earthquakes_in_the_Levant#cite_note-12

[77] Williams, J., M. Schwab and A. Brauer. 2011. An early first-century earthquake in the Dead Sea". International Geology Review. 54 (10): 1219.

calendar seven out of every nineteen years."[78] It may seem strange to us to occasionally add a 13th month for timekeeping but it worked.

The moon completes one cycle around the Earth every 29.5 days. Passover <u>always</u> fell on a full moon[79] because it was such an important event that it was synchronized to the lunar cycle: *"On the fourteenth day of the first month the Lord's Passover is to be held."* Numbers 28:16. Jesus was crucified on the Friday before Passover: *"Then the Jewish leaders took Jesus from Caiaphas to the palace of the Roman governor. By now it was early morning, and to avoid ceremonial uncleanness they did not enter the palace, because they wanted to be able to eat the Passover."* John 18:28.

Did a solar eclipse occur? *"From noon until three in the afternoon darkness came over all the land."* Matthew 27:45. Some people believe that there was a solar eclipse when Jesus died and cite 3 April 33 A.D. as the day for the eclipse. There was a partial weak eclipse on that day. [80] But a partial eclipse doesn't match the Biblical description of the darkness or the Jewish tradition of Passover falling on a full moon. A solar eclipse on a full moon is astronomically impossible.

[78] http://www.crivoice.org/calendar.html
[79] https://www.chabad.org/holidays/passover/pesach_cdo/aid/4250850/jewish/Why-Is-Passover-on-a-Full-Moon.htm
[80] https://biblearchaeology.org/research/the-daniel-9-24-27-project/4360-how-the-passover-illuminates-the-date-of-the-crucifixion

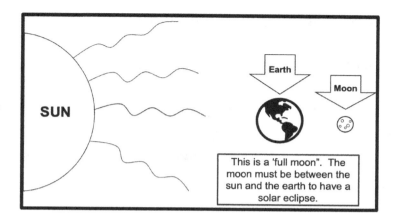

This drawing shows the moon's position during a full moon when Jesus was crucified. The moon is on the wrong side of the Earth for a solar eclipse! The moon must be between the sun and the Earth to create a solar eclipse and it takes about two weeks for the moon to make that journey.

There is evidence outside of the Bible for this darkness. Phlegon, a Greek historian from 137 A.D., wrote, *"It became night in the sixth hour of the day so that stars even appeared in the heavens."* [81] The *"stars even appeared in the Heavens,"* so it was very dark. The maximum duration of total darkness in an eclipse is about seven minutes[82] and the Biblical account says it was dark for three hours. Phlegon also recorded that there was <u>an eclipse during a full moon</u>.[83]

---

[81] https://www.neverthirsty.org/about-christ/historical-quotes/phlegon/

[82] https://www.christianevidence.net/2017/12/historical-evidence-darkness-earthquake.html

[83] https://en.wikipedia.org/wiki/Crucifixion_darkness

There is no astronomical explanation for the darkness described in the Bible. This couldn't have been a naturally occurring eclipse. The moon's lunar cycle around the Earth affects the tides in the ocean. If God had moved the moon to create a solar eclipse, there would have been tidal effects worldwide. We don't read about that inside or outside of the Bible. This was an act of God.

HOW WAS JESUS'S BODY PROCESSED?

Two men- Joseph of Arimathea and the Pharisee Nicodemus- retrieved the dead body of Jesus and processed it for burial. *"Later, Joseph of Arimathea asked Pilate for the body of Jesus. Now Joseph was a disciple of Jesus, but secretly because he feared the Jewish leaders. With Pilate's permission, he came and took the body away. He was accompanied by Nicodemus, the man who earlier had visited Jesus at night. Nicodemus brought a mixture of myrrh and aloes, about seventy-five pounds. Taking Jesus' body, the two of them wrapped it, with the spices, in strips of linen. This was in accordance with Jewish burial customs. At the place where Jesus was crucified, there was a garden, and in the garden a new tomb, in which no one had ever been laid. Because it was the Jewish day of Preparation and since the tomb was nearby, they laid Jesus there."* John 19:38-41.

Who was Joseph of Arimathea and why was he allowed to have Jesus' body? Joseph was referred to as 'Nobilis Decurio' or Minister of Mines by the Roman government. He may have already known Pontius Pilate because of his designation. Arimathea is modern-day Ramallah, Israel, and is eight miles from Jerusalem. Joseph was supposedly the owner of tin mines and was wealthy enough to have a rich person's tomb. He was allegedly the uncle of Mary, the mother of Jesus.[84] This explains why Pilate would have released Jesus' body to Joseph, for it is usually released to a relative.

Joseph and Nicodemus were members of the Sanhedrin, the ruling religious body in Jerusalem. Nicodemus was a Pharisee, so he was a teacher of the Torah. Jesus referred to Nicodemus as 'Israel's teacher' (John 3:10), indicating Nicodemus' stature. Nicodemus brought 75 lbs. of myrrh and aloe. This was more than three times normal and was usually reserved for the bodies of kings.

Jesus' body would have been washed and oiled, according to the Jewish Mishnah: *"According to Jewish custom, the body was washed and straightened, then wrapped tightly from the armpits to the ankles in strips of linen about a foot wide. The gummy aromatic spices were placed between the wrappings or folds of the*

---

[84] https://joan-berry.com/
what-you-may-not-know-about-joseph-of-arimathea/

linen partly as a preservative and partly as a cement to glue the linen cloths into a solid covering which adhered so closely to the body that it would not easily be removed. The aloes were a fragrant wood which was pounded to a dry dust, and the myrrh was an aromatic gum which was mixed in with the dry aloes. The powder immediately around the myrrh would become sticky and would cement the linen cloths to each other and to the body, but the bulk of the aloe powder would most likely remain dry. The face was covered with a cloth napkin or handkerchief which was sometimes wrapped fully around the head." [85]

There is a lot of detail in that quote:

- The body was wrapped tightly in linen.
- Gummy spices were placed between the wrappings.
- Myrrh and 'Aloe wood' were used.
- The face was covered with a cloth.

'Aloe' is not the succulent Aloe we think of today; it is agarwood.[86] This aromatic wood is also known as *"Wood of the Gods"* and its *"heartwood becomes very dense, dark, and saturated with resin."*[87] Myrrh is an aromatic resin that has antiseptic properties[88] and

---

[85] https://evidenceforchristianity.org/a-muslim-friend-claims-anointing-with-myrrh-and-aloe-is-not-a-jewish-practice-is-this-truer/

[86] https://grandawood.com.au/blogs/news/82887686-agarwood-mentioned-in-bible

[87] https://en.wikipedia.org/wiki/Agarwood

[88] https://en.wikipedia.org/wiki/Myrrh

appears to kill parasites.[89] Myrrh likely repels insects,[90] which could be the reason why it was used. Flies quickly found dead bodies in a warm climate such as Jerusalem in April, when Jesus died. Jewish tradition dictated that a relative viewed the dead loved one three days after death. No one wanted to see their dead loved one covered with maggots. Wrapping a body with linen strips and then using a mixture of agarwood and myrrh would preserve the body. It would also reduce the likelihood of maggots eating the deceased loved one.

Did Joseph and Nicodemus wrap Jesus and use this mixture? It was getting late in the day when they recovered Jesus' body, and some people might argue that they rushed things. This doesn't make sense. Both men revered Jesus and certainly wouldn't have wanted Jesus' body infested with carrion beetles and maggots.

The myrrh-agarwood mixture would be sticky. It would also be aromatic and would taste bitter because the root word for myrrh means bitter. Unwrapping a body covered with this would be a nasty task, as we shall discuss later.

---

[89] https://volantaroma.com/blogs/guides/myrrh-essential-oil-guide
[90] https://www.happypreppers.com/myrrh.html

WERE THERE ROMAN GUARDS AT THE TOMB?

There were at least four guards at Jesus' tomb and perhaps eight.

"The next day, the one after Preparation Day, the chief priests and the Pharisees went to Pilate. 'Sir,' they said, 'we remember that while he was still alive that deceiver said, 'After three days I will rise again.' So give the order for the tomb to be made secure until the third day'...'Take a guard,' Pilate answered. 'Go, make the tomb as secure as you know how.' So they went and made the tomb secure by putting a seal on the stone and posting the guard." Matthew 27:62-65.

The smallest unit of organization in the Roman army was called a Contubernium and it consisted of eight soldiers.[91] A Roman guard was half of a Contubernium or four soldiers. Each soldier would be on guard for four or six hours, and then the next one would be on guard duty. This enabled the unit to guard something for days or weeks if needed. If two guards were on duty at the tomb, then two of these 4-guard units were on duty. Recall that the punishment was death for a Roman soldier who fell asleep while on guard duty. No guard slept, as the story goes, *"When the chief priests had met with the elders and devised a plan, they gave*

---

[91] https://imperiumromanum.pl/en/roman-army/units-of-roman-army/contubernium/#google_vignette

the soldiers a large sum of money, telling them, *"You are to say, 'His disciples came during the night and stole him away while we were asleep.' 'If this report gets to the governor, we will satisfy him and keep you out of trouble.' So the soldiers took the money and did as they were instructed."* Matthew 28:12-15.

The above verse says, "...*stole him away while we were asleep.*" Does this make sense? No. As previously stated, a sleeping guard was a soon-to-be-executed one. The story must have sounded ridiculous to the people in Jerusalem. It would have heightened the interest in Jesus.

Peter and John went into the tomb and saw something interesting: *"Then Simon Peter came, following him, and went into the tomb. He saw the linen cloths lying there, and the face cloth, which had been on Jesus' head, not lying with the linen cloths but folded up in a place by itself."* John 20:6-8 ESV. They saw:

- The linen wrappings (with the myrrh and agarwood resin mixtures) laying there.
- The face cloth folded up.

Who unwraps a dead body before stealing it, and especially a body that has smelly and sticky resin on the linen? Wouldn't it make more sense to grab it and go? Removing the burial wrappings was sacrilegious to the Jews! Jesus' disciples and followers were

Jews, so we can confidently say that the body wasn't unwrapped and stolen.

Another amazing aspect of this story is that the thief would have to be overly neat because he or she folded the face cloth! He or she left the wrappings in a heap but folded the face cloth. This is illogical and nonsensical.

DID MARY MAGDALENE VISIT THE WRONG TOMB?

Some people believe that Mary Magdalene and others went to the wrong tomb and that is why the tomb was empty. Joseph of Arimathea's tomb was a rich person's tomb because it had a rolling stone. Less expensive tombs had a square or rectangular stone that fit into a similar opening in the tomb. Mary Magdalene and the other women knew where this tomb was: *"The women who had come with Jesus from Galilee followed Joseph and saw the tomb and how his body was laid in it."* Luke 23:55. It would have been almost impossible to mistake it for any other tomb because it was a rich person's tomb that soldiers guarded.

This happened after three days: *"There was a violent earthquake, for an angel of the Lord came down from heaven and, going to the tomb, rolled back the stone and sat on it. His appearance was like lightning, and his clothes were white as snow. The guards were so afraid of him that they shook and became like dead men."* Matthew 28:2-4.

PART 3: ANALYSIS

We again have no replicated data but we do have quite a bit of reported observations. Those observations can be used with today's knowledge to understand what happened to Jesus. For example, we benefit from vastly more detailed medical knowledge today. No one knew about hypovolemic shock or pericardial effusions back then. They didn't know how excessive blood loss affected the vital organs and how a heart attack is an inevitable result of continued blood loss. We can assess the damage done by beatings plus a scourging plus a crown of thorns plus a crucifixion plus being stabbed by a spear, and medically conclude that Jesus died.

The climate in ancient Jerusalem might have been slightly cooler than today.[92] Jesus was crucified in April. Jesus' body would have cooled after death. Joseph and Nicodemus would have recognized that Jesus was dead by his lack of body warmth, lack

[92] https://blog.adw.org/2014/07/
what-was-the-climate-and-weather-of-israel-like-at-the-time-of-jesus/

of breathing, lack of bleeding from all his wounds, accumulation of fluids in his legs, and his discoloration. This is why they wrapped his body. He indeed was dead.

Geologists review the damage and historical accounts to determine a range of dates for an ancient earthquake.[93] This is how geologists know that an earthquake occurred in the general area of Israel. It left telltale signs in the geological strata, and there were also accounts of it from Roman sources. The geological strata are physical data that other scientists can review and the Roman sources affirm that an earthquake did occur. These are satisfying data.

The astronomical location of the moon during a solar eclipse is well known, as the Passover occurs during a full moon. It isn't astronomically possible for a solar eclipse to occur during a full moon, but it did. It was a Heavenly event that science cannot explain.

The torn curtain was about 60 feet tall, 30 feet wide, and about 3 to 4 inches thick. There isn't a scientific explanation of how such a curtain could be torn from top to bottom.

The Roman Army was a highly disciplined, professional army. For example, senior officers in a Roman legion would punish cohorts that underperformed by using

---

[93] https://slate.com/news-and-politics/2010/01/how-do-they-measure-earthquakes-from-250-years-ago.html

'decimation,' which required the cohort to kill every 10th man in the unit.[94] The person to be killed was selected by casting lots. The idea that Roman soldiers fell asleep when someone supposedly stole Jesus' body is nonsensical because the penalty for that is the execution of the guard. Locals in Jerusalem would find such an accusation laughable.

It was sacrilegious for a Jew to unwrap a dead body so no Jews unwrapped and stole Jesus' body. No one would unwrap a dead body with gummy and smelly resin on it and then fold the cloth headpiece. These are two opposite actions.

---

[94] https://en.wikipedia.org/wiki/Decimation_(punishment)

SUMMARY

1. Jesus very likely suffered from hypovolemic shock caused by a tremendous number of wounds. He probably had a pericardial effusion and perhaps a pleural (i.e., lung) effusion. He died from all his wounds and loss of blood.
2. A Roman soldier ensured that he was dead by stabbing him with a spear, most likely in the heart. The pericardial sac (or the pleural sac) ruptured, causing clear plasma and blood to drain from the wound.
3. There was an earthquake.

4. The sky went dark for hours. It is astronomically impossible for it to have been a normal solar eclipse.
5. The guards did not dare fall asleep for fear of execution. No Jew would unwrap Jesus' dead body and remove it from the tomb because it is sacrilegious to do so. It is illogical to unwrap a dead body and then fold the headpiece.

PART 4: DATA ABOUT THE RESURRECTION

We again have oral history data to analyze for the resurrection. We also, tellingly, have medical facts.

Did Jesus Rise From the Dead?

The Apostles wrote that Jesus appeared to more than 500 people for over a month after He rose from the dead. Below are the events as recorded in the New Testament:

- **APPEARS TO MARY MAGDALENE:** *"At this, she turned around and saw Jesus standing there, but she did not realize that it was Jesus. He asked her, 'Woman, why are you crying? Who is it you are looking for?' Thinking he was the gardener, she said, 'Sir, if you have carried him away, tell me where you have put him, and I will get him.' Jesus said to her, 'Mary.' She turned toward him and cried out in Aramaic, 'Rabboni!' (which means 'Teacher')."* John 20:14-16.
- **APPEARS TO TWO MEN ON ROAD TO EMMAUS:** *"Now that same day two of them were going to a village called Emmaus, about seven miles from Jerusalem... As they talked*

and discussed these things with each other, Jesus himself came up and walked along with them; but they were kept from recognizing him." Luke 24:13-16.

- **APPEARS TO THE APOSTLES:** *"While they were still talking about this, Jesus himself stood among them and said to them, 'Peace be with you.'"* Luke 24:36.

- **APPEARS TO APOSTLES WITH THOMAS PRESENT:** *"Now Thomas (also known as Didymus), one of the Twelve, was not with the disciples when Jesus came. So the other disciples told him, 'We have seen the Lord!' But he said to them, 'Unless I see the nail marks in his hands and put my finger where the nails were, and put my hand into his side, I will not believe.' A week later his disciples were in the house again, and Thomas was with them. Though the doors were locked, Jesus came and stood among them and said, 'Peace be with you!'"* John 20:24-26.

- **APPEARS TO APOSTLES ON SHORE OF SEA OF GALILEE:** *"Afterward Jesus appeared again to his disciples, by the Sea of Galilee. It happened this way: Simon Peter, Thomas (also known as Didymus), Nathanael from Cana in Galilee, the sons of Zebedee, and two other disciples were together. 'I'm going out to fish,' Simon Peter told them, and they said, 'We'll go with you.' ...Early in the morning, Jesus stood on* the shore, but the disciples did not realize that it was Jesus...Then the disciple whom Jesus loved said to Peter, 'It is the Lord!'" John 21:1-7.

- **SEEN BY PETER (CEPHAS), 500 BELIEVERS, AND THEN JAMES:** *"For what I received I passed on to you as of first importance: that Christ died for our sins according to the Scriptures, that he was buried, that he was raised on the third day according to the Scriptures, and that he appeared to Cephas, and then to the Twelve. After that, he appeared to more than five hundred of the brothers and sisters at the same time, most of whom are still living, though some have fallen asleep. Then he appeared to James, then to all the apostles, and last of all he appeared to me also, as to one abnormally born."* 1 Corinthians 15:3-8.

- **APPEARS TO DISCIPLES, ASCENDED TO HEAVEN:** *"When he had led them out to the vicinity of Bethany, he lifted up his hands and blessed them. While he was blessing them, he left them and was taken up into heaven. Then they worshiped him and returned to Jerusalem with great joy. And they stayed continually at the temple, praising God."* Luke 24:50-53.

- **JESUS APPEARED TO PEOPLE FOR 40 DAYS:** *"In my former book, Theophilus, I wrote about all that Jesus began to do and to teach until the day he was taken up to heaven, after giving instructions through the Holy Spirit to the* *apostles he had chosen. After his suffering, he presented himself to them and gave many convincing proofs that he was alive. He appeared to them over a period of forty days and spoke about the kingdom of God."* Acts 1:1-3.

- **JESUS APPEARED TO PAUL, ON THE ROAD TO DAMASCUS YEARS LATER:** *"Then he appeared to James, then to all the apostles, and last of all he appeared to me also, as to one abnormally born."* 1 Corinthians 15:7-8.

Readers can make three important observations about these appearances. First, Jesus appeared to more than 500 people over a period of 40 days. That is a lot of people and a long time. The appearances were inside, outside on a road, on the shore, and in a small and large group. There were many appearances and witnesses.

The second important observation is that no one claimed this person wasn't Jesus. Something absent can be significant and that is the case here. No one recants Jesus' resurrection inside or outside of the Bible. Paul makes the point in 1 Corinthians 15 that *"most of whom are still living."* These people could have disputed Jesus' resurrection if it were false, but none did. The Pharisees and Sadducees would have loved to have someone say that Jesus' resurrection was a lie. They'd have loved saying, *"EXTRA! EXTRA! Read all about it! Apostles made the resurrection up!"*

More than 500 people would not change their story. This is credible evidence that the resurrection is true.

The third important observation is that the Apostles' behavior totally changed after the resurrection. The Apostles justifiably feared for their lives after Jesus was crucified. They could be next, after all. *"On the evening of that day, the first day of the week, the doors being locked where the disciples were for fear of the Jews, Jesus came and stood among them and said to them, 'Peace be with you.'"* John 20:19. The Apostles were fearful and hiding behind locked doors.

They behaved differently after the resurrection. The Temple guards and the Sadducees seized John and Peter and brought them before the Sanhedrin. Then, John and Peter were commanded not to teach or speak about Jesus. A fearful person who was afraid for his life might say, *"Yes, sir"* and leave. That is not what happened: *"But Peter and John replied, 'Which is right in God's eyes: to listen to you, or to him? You be the judges! As for us, we cannot help speaking about what we have seen and heard.'"* Acts 4:19-20. Of the 12 Apostles, 11 met with violent deaths. How each one died is not known, but scholars think that...

- Peter was crucified upside down.
- Andrew was crucified on an X-shaped cross.[95]

---

[95] https://www.christianity.com/church/church-history/timeline/1-300/whatever-happened-to-the-twelve-apostles-11629558.html

- Matthew was put to death by the sword.[96]
- James the brother of Jesus was thrown from the top of a temple to the ground. He survived the fall and was beaten to death by people with clubs.
- Bartholomew was flayed to death by a whip.
- Thomas was stabbed to death with a spear in India.
- Emperor Nero beheaded Paul.
- Matthias, who was selected after Judas Iscariot died, was stoned and then beheaded.
- John was boiled in oil but survived.

Why would the Apostles die for a lie? Why would the Apostles change from being afraid to being so fearless that they would be crucified, stabbed, flayed to death, beheaded, or boiled in oil? What changed?

This is what changed: they saw Jesus ascend to Heaven. *"He said to them: '…But you will receive power when the Holy Spirit comes on you; and you will be my witnesses in Jerusalem, and in all Judea and Samaria, and to the ends of the earth.' After he said this, he was taken up before their very eyes, and a cloud hid him from their sight. They were looking intently up into the sky as he was going, when suddenly two men dressed in white stood beside them. 'Men of Galilee,' they said, 'why do you stand here looking into the sky? This same Jesus, who has been taken from*

---

[96] https://www.gotquestions.org/apostles-die.html

you into heaven, will come back in the same way you have seen him go into heaven.'" Acts 1:7-10.

The number of events, number of witnesses (500+), and time frame of 40 days clearly show that a man named Jesus was alive. There are too many people to dismiss over too much time. This leads to the next important question.

Is the Resurrection of Jesus Real?

It is time to answer this question. There are only two possibilities:

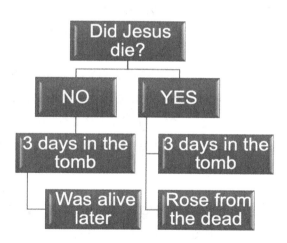

Jesus either did or didn't die. In either case, Jesus spent three days in a tomb sealed by the Pharisees and Sadducees. Then many people saw Jesus over 40 days, in many distinct locations.

JESUS DIDN'T DIE: You've already read how devastating his wounds were, how he suffered tremendous blood loss, and how his last wound was from a spear to most likely his heart. Then, Jesus must have been so wholly unconscious that he never groaned or moved once while he was wrapped with linen and the resins applied. The wrapping, especially the resins, would have stung as they touched his wounds. Jesus was carried to the tomb and He was sealed shut in it for three days without food and water. His body would have craved water...remember, "*I thirst.*" At the end of those three days, we are now supposed to believe that this man's body healed itself so much that he regained consciousness, somehow unwrapped himself, and walked out without aid. The hand, foot, and spear wounds were still there but somehow not bleeding anymore. He was fine.

Does this make any sense to you? It goes against all that we know about medicine and the human body. It is such an incredible story that it borders on science fiction. I don't see how any rational human being can believe this.

JESUS DIED: Everything that we know about what happened to Jesus says that he died. You've read about Jesus' torture, his wounds, his horrific blood loss, his being stabbed with a spear, the processing of his body, and how he was sealed into a tomb for three days. His wounds were massive and his medical care was nonexistent. The guards would have been severely punished and perhaps executed if he were left alive on the cross.

There is an example of Roman guards being killed in the Book of Acts. The Roman King Herod imprisoned the Apostle Paul: *"After arresting him, he put him in prison, handing him over to be guarded by four squads of four soldiers each. Herod intended to bring him out for public trial after the Passover."* Acts 12:4. This text says, *"four squads of four guards each."* Two guard units from two Contuberniums were used in this case. An Angel of the Lord rescued Paul and he left the prison. What happened to the guards? *"After Herod had a thorough search made for him and did not find him, he cross-examined the guards and ordered that they be executed."* Acts 12:19. Herod had the guards executed.

No, Jesus wasn't alive on the cross. The guards were certain that Jesus was dead, particularly after inflicting a spear thrust to him. Blood and water came out, but no text in or outside the New Testament describes pumping blood. No pumping blood, no heartbeat. He was dead.

People may suggest that Jesus died and a double- an actor- substituted for Jesus so that we'd believe in God. Jesus appeared to James, his half-brother (1 Corinthians 15:7). James would have known if this was an imposter. Jerusalem was a small city at the time of Jesus, and he was a well-known figure. They knew what he looked like and sounded like. The actor would have had to impersonate Jesus and fool over 500 people for 40 days. Who could do that? This would be the most outstanding actor ever to impersonate Jesus for that long. Not only that, but the actor would have somehow been *"...taken up into heaven."* Luke 24:51.

It is a ridiculous idea.

Jesus died, and then He rose from the dead.

What can we Learn from Mary, Jesus' Mother?

There is ample evidence that Jesus is real and the Son of God. Are you convinced yet? I hope so! But if you are not, let's review what Jesus' mother went through.

Simeon warned Mary about her future: *"The child's father and mother marveled at what was said about him. Then Simeon blessed them and said to Mary, his mother: 'This child is destined to cause the falling and rising of many in Israel, and to be a sign that will be spoken against, so that the thoughts of many hearts will be revealed. And a sword will pierce your own soul too.'"* Luke 2:33-35.

"A sword will pierce your own soul too." Was Mary at Jesus' scourging? The Bible text doesn't say. It seems

likely that she was. Why would she miss it? Many Roman Catholics believe that Mary attended Jesus' scourging because of 'The Dolorous Passion of our Lord Jesus Christ'[97]; many also believe that the risen Jesus met with his mother Mary.[98] If she was there, then Mary would have seen her son stripped naked and chained to a post like he was a criminal. She would have seen the soldier pick up the flagrum and start beating her son with it. Mary would have seen bits of skin, muscle, connective tissue, organs, and bones torn off and flying. Then she would have seen gushes of blood…so much that she could smell it if she were close enough. In the end, she could have seen a soldier throw salt onto her son's wounds and then lead him away. Seeing that would be like a sword piercing your own soul, I think.

The next time that Mary could have seen her son was when he was brought out to carry the cross to Golgotha, where he was crucified. She would have been <u>stunned</u> by his appearance. The crown of thorns on his head would have caused a lot of bleeding and his body would have been a torn and bloody mess. He was beaten in the face so much he was hard to recognize: *"Just as there were many who were appalled at him, his appearance was so disfigured beyond that of any*

[97] https://www.documentacatholicaomnia.eu/03d/1774-1824,_ Emmerich._Anne_Catherine,_Dolorous_Passion_Of_Our_Lord_Jesus_ Christ,_EN.pdf
[98] https://crisismagazine.com/opinion/ did-the-resurrected-christ-appear-to-his-blessed-mother

human being...." Isaiah 52:14. She might have seen spittle running down his face from the guards who beat him. She clearly saw how much weaker he was and how he needed help with carrying the patibulum (cross piece) from Simon of Cyrene. Then, she saw the soldiers use nails that were the size of spikes to affix her son to the cross. Jesus was naked and dying from the cumulative effect of all his wounds. We know that Mary was at the crucifixion because Jesus talked to her from the cross: *"When Jesus saw his mother and the disciple whom he loved standing nearby, he said to his mother, 'Woman, behold, your son!' Then he said to the disciple, 'Behold, your mother!' And from that hour the disciple took her to his own home."* John 19:26-27. All that she could do was to stand there...and watch.

Mary was a devout Jew and she *"... treasured up all these things and pondered them in her heart"* when someone called her child the Messiah (Luke 2:19). There were at least seven such incidents:

- An angel visited Mary before her conception.
- An angel appeared to Joseph, her husband, in a dream.
- Shepherds described an angel to Mary and Joseph.
- Wise men worshipped her son.
- Mary marveled at Simeon's and Anna's blessings when Jesus was eight days old.

- An angel told her husband Joseph to go to Egypt.
- An angel told Joseph to return to Israel.

Now, Mary just saw her son die. That didn't match what she believed from the incidents. Did she have doubts?

Did Jesus appear to his mother and half-brothers after He rose from the dead? There is indirect evidence that he did. His half-brothers James and Judas (i.e., Jude in the New Testament) became believers and they wrote two of the books in the New Testament. Mary was probably in the room[99] when the Holy Spirit came to each of them ten days after Jesus' death: *"When the day of Pentecost came, they were all together in one place. Suddenly a sound like the blowing of a violent wind came from heaven and filled the whole house where they were sitting. They saw what seemed to be tongues of fire that separated and came to rest on each of them. All of them were filled with the Holy Spirit and began to speak in other tongues as the Spirit enabled them."* Acts 2:1-4. So, Mary was an integral part of the believers.

We've already shown that Jesus appeared to more than 500 people on multiple occasions over 40 days. I have a tough time believing that a resurrected Jesus met with all those people but not with his mother.

---

[99] https://carm.org/about-people/was-mary-in-the-upper-room-during-pentecost-when-the-holy-spirit-was-poured-out/

Before Jesus was arrested, his family thought that he was out of his mind! In Mark 3:20-21, we read, *"Then Jesus entered a house, and again a crowd gathered, so that he and his disciples were not even able to eat. When his family heard about this, they went to take charge of him, for they said, 'He is out of his mind.'"* What changed for her and her sons James and Jude?

James and Jude initially thought that Jesus was out of his mind. Then, they became such strong believers that they were martyred for their faith. Perhaps Jesus did appear to his family.

If Mary saw her resurrected son, how would she have reacted? Would she have fallen on her knees, grasped his legs, and cried? Would she have looked at Jesus and then said, *"How?"* She would have wanted to know how he could be alive and standing before her with holes in his wrists and feet and with a large hole in his side from a Roman spear thrust. *"How? How is this possible?"*

Jesus answered that question for the two apostles on the road to Emmaus after Jesus was resurrected. They didn't recognize him. The apostles were trying to make sense of Jesus' crucifixion. Jesus said, *"'Did not the Messiah have to suffer these things and then enter his glory?' And beginning with Moses and all the Prophets, he explained to them what was said in all the Scriptures concerning himself."* Luke 24:26-27. If He explained how He fulfilled the scriptures for his disciples, perhaps he did this for his mother and two half-brothers.

PART 4: ANALYSIS

The death and resurrection of Jesus is like the accounts about the airplanes flying into the Twin Towers on 9-11. We have the advantage of television and cell phone images to re-live that terrible day. Without those, we would have just personal accounts of the event. The death and resurrection of Jesus is similar.

There is a conclusive case for Jesus's death. As for Jesus' resurrection, more than 500 saw a resurrected Jesus. He was seen inside, outside, at various locations, and over 40 days. Taken collectively, the oral data are compelling in the New Testament. SOMEONE did walk about and claim to be Jesus. It was Jesus and not an imposter.

Jesus' mother Mary was an eyewitness to the excessive brutality and cruelty of the Roman regime. She probably was at his scourging and was at his crucifixion. Given that Jesus appeared to so many people it seems highly likely that she saw her son. Could an actor playing the part of Jesus fool her? Could the actor sustain the part for 40 days, fool the

Apostles, and fool so many? It would take the most outstanding actor of all time to do that.

SUMMARY

1. Jesus died.
2. Hundreds saw someone claiming to be Jesus for over a month.
3. Of the more than 500 people who saw this person, no one denied that it was Jesus. There are no stories of recanting inside or outside of the New Testament.
4. Jesus appeared to his half-brother James, who would have recognized if it wasn't Jesus.
5. All Apostles except John were executed for their beliefs, and some of the executions were brutal. None recanted. Hundreds of early Christians were persecuted for their beliefs and none recanted. This is compelling evidence.
6. The Apostles' behavior changed 180 degrees from timidity to fearlessness when preaching the Gospel due to seeing Jesus after he died.
7. Collectively, these data affirm the New Testament account that Jesus rose from the dead.

PART 5: PROPHETIC AND MATHEMATICAL DATA

Old Testament Prophesies That Jesus Fulfilled

What Old Testament scriptures did Jesus recite to his disciples to explain that he is the Son of God? The scriptures had to be in the Old Testament.

Below are 25 unique prophecies in the Old Testament... ones that Jesus could have recited. You will see below a PROPHECY and then a FULFILLMENT of the prophecy. The prophecies are listed in chronological order based on Jesus' life. Every prophecy was made at least 400 years before Jesus was born. Biblical scholars acknowledge that Jewish prophets authored the books in the Old Testament hundreds to thousands of years before Jesus.

At the end of these prophecies, I calculate the mathematical probability that these occurred by other events. That answer will surprise you.

#	PROPHECY	FULFILLMENT
1.	*"In the beginning, God created the Heavens and the earth."* Genesis 1:1.	Genesis was written over 3,000 years ago. This verse was originally written in Hebrew, and the word 'Elohim' was used for the English word 'God.' 'Elohim' is plural, so it means 'we.' Who is 'we'? In John 10:30, Jesus said, *"I and the father are one."* Jesus also said, *"Very truly I tell you, before Abraham was born, I am."* John 8:58. There are various dates for Abraham's birth, but all are at least 1,700 years before Jesus was born. Jesus said that he was alive 1,700 years before he was even born! Also, the *"I am"* is significant. God said to Moses, "Say this to the people of Israel, *'I AM has sent me to you.'"* Exodus 3:14. Jesus said that he is *"I am"* and thus is God.
2.	*"Then God said, 'Yes, but your wife Sarah will bear you a son, and you will call him Isaac. I will establish my covenant with him as an everlasting covenant for his descendants after him.'"* Genesis 17:19.	This is another verse from Genesis. God tells Abraham that He will establish an eternal binding relationship with Abraham and the progeny of his son Isaac. Jesus is a direct descendant of Isaac: *"... the son of Jacob, the son of Isaac, the son of Abraham, the son of Terah, the son of Nahor...."* Luke 3:34. This prophecy was fulfilled through Jesus.

3.	*"'The days are coming,' declares the Lord, 'when I will raise up for David a righteous Branch, a King who will reign wisely and do what is just and right in the land. In his days Judah will be saved and Israel will live in safety. This is the name by which he will be called: The Lord Our Righteous Savior.'"* Jeremiah 23:5-6.	The Book of Jeremiah was written about 550 B.C. Jesus was a direct descendant of King David. In the New Testament, Luke wrote that Jesus was *"...the son of Melea, the son of Menna, the son of Mattatha, the son of Nathan, the son of David, the son of Jesse, the son of Obed, the son of Boaz, the son of Salmon, the son of Nahshon..."* Luke 3:31-32. Should we believe this ancestry from the New Testament? Yes. Luke is likely recording Jesus' legal lineage while Matthew records Jesus' biological lineage.
4.	*"But you, Bethlehem Ephrathah, though you are small among the clans of Judah, out of you will come for me one who will be ruler over Israel, whose origins are from of old, from ancient times."* Micah 5:2.	Micah was written between 750 to 687 B.C. Jesus was indeed born in Bethlehem: *"After Jesus was born in Bethlehem in Judea, during the time of King Herod, Magi from the east came to Jerusalem ..."* Matthew 2:1. Bethlehem was in the district of Ephrathah and was a village of about 200-400 people at the time of Jesus' birth. So, this prophecy was specific.

5.	*"I see him, but not now; I behold him, but not near. A star will come out of Jacob; a scepter will rise out of Israel."* Numbers 24:17.	This was a 3,000-year-old prophecy of Balaam. The star is about Jesus. Matthew 2:1-2 says, *"After Jesus was born in Bethlehem in Judea, during the time of King Herod, Magi from the east came to Jerusalem and asked, 'Where is the one who has been born king of the Jews? We saw his star when it rose and have come to worship him.'"* This is a quote from the wise men who followed a star to Bethlehem and found the Messiah Jesus in a manger.
6.	*"Therefore the Lord himself will give you a sign: The virgin will conceive and give birth to a son, and will call him Immanuel."* Isaiah 7:14.	This is quite a prophecy! A virgin giving birth to a baby would have been a miracle when this was written, over 700 years before Jesus was born. It is possible today through in vitro fertilization. According to the New Testament, Jesus <u>was</u> born of a virgin. *"'How will this be,' Mary asked the angel, 'since I am a virgin?' The angel answered, 'The Holy Spirit will come on you, and the power of the Most High will overshadow you. So the holy one to be born will be called the Son of God.'"* Luke 1:34-35.
7.	*"When Israel was a child, I loved him, and out of*	The Book of Hosea was written about 700 B.C. Jesus was indeed taken to Egypt. *"When they*

	Egypt I called my son." Hosea 11:1.	*had gone, an angel of the Lord appeared to Joseph in a dream. 'Get up,' he said, 'take the child and his mother and escape to Egypt. Stay there until I tell you, for Herod is going to search for the child to kill him.' So he got up, took the child and his mother during the night and left for Egypt, where he stayed until the death of Herod. And so was fulfilled what the Lord had said through the prophet: 'Out of Egypt I called my son.'" Matthew 2:13-15.*
8.	*"This is what the Lord says: 'A voice is heard in Ramah, mourning and great weeping, Rachel weeping for her children and refusing to be comforted, because they are no more.'"* Jeremiah 31:15.	This verse prophesizes that a terrible event will occur where children will be killed in Ramah, which is just a few miles from Jerusalem. *"When Herod realized that he had been outwitted by the Magi, he was furious, and he gave orders to kill all the boys in Bethlehem and its vicinity who were two years old and under, in accordance with the time he had learned from the Magi."* Matthew 2:16. Notice the, *"and its vicinity"* phrase.
9.	*"A voice of one calling: 'In the wilderness prepare the way for the Lord; make straight in the*	John the Baptist was the voice in the wilderness. He was a prophet who preceded Jesus and prepared the way by baptizing people. *"In those days John the Baptist came, preaching in the wilderness of*

	desert a highway for our God.'" Isaiah 40:3.	Judea and saying, 'Repent, for the kingdom of heaven has come near.' This is he who was spoken of through the prophet Isaiah: 'A voice of one calling in the wilderness, "Prepare the way for the Lord, make straight paths for him."' Matthew 3:1-3.
10.	"Here is my servant, whom I uphold, my chosen one in whom I delight; I will put my Spirit on him, and he will bring justice to the nations." Isaiah 42:1.	This ancient prophecy describes how God will bless his chosen one with his Spirit. Luke describes this event. "When all the people were being baptized, Jesus was baptized too. And as he was praying, heaven was opened and the Holy Spirit descended on him in bodily form like a dove. And a voice came from heaven: 'You are my Son, whom I love; with you I am well pleased.'" Luke 3:21-22.
11.	"Nevertheless, there will be no more gloom for those who were in distress. In the past he humbled the land of Zebulun and the land of Naphtali, but in the future he will honor Galilee of the nations, by the Way of the	This prophecy says that Galilee will be honored. Jesus' ministry was centered in and around Galilee. "When Jesus heard that John had been put in prison, he withdrew to Galilee. Leaving Nazareth, he went and lived in Capernaum, which was by the lake in the area of Zebulun and Naphtali." Matthew 4:12-13.

	Sea, beyond the Jordan..." Isaiah 9:1.	
12.	"'...Be strong, do not fear; your God will come, he will come with vengeance; with divine retribution he will come to save you.' Then will the eyes of the blind be opened and the ears of the deaf unstopped. Then will the lame leap like a deer, and the mute tongue shout for joy." Isaiah 35:4-6.	This is another ancient verse that predicts that God will open the eyes of the blind, the ears of the deaf and that the lame will walk. Jesus fulfilled this prophecy. "Jesus replied, 'Go back and report to John what you hear and see: The blind receive sight, the lame walk, those who have leprosy are cleansed, the deaf hear, the dead are raised, and the good news is proclaimed to the poor.'" Matthew 11:4-5.
13.	"For I endure scorn for your sake, and shame covers my face. I am a foreigner to my own family, a stranger to my own mother's children; for zeal for your house consumes me, and the insults of those who insult	The Psalms were written about 1,000 B.C. Jesus became angry when he saw the money changers and the greedy sellers of animals for sacrifice in the Temple. Zeal for God's house did consume him. "In the temple courts he found people selling cattle, sheep and doves, and others sitting at tables exchanging money. So he made a whip out of cords, and drove all from the temple courts, both sheep and cattle; he scattered the coins

	you fall on me." Psalm 69:7-9.	*of the money changers and overturned their tables. To those who sold doves he said, 'Get these out of here! Stop turning my Father's house into a market!'"* John 2:14-16.
14.	*"Rejoice greatly, Daughter Zion! Shout, Daughter Jerusalem! See, your king comes to you, righteous and victorious, lowly and riding on a donkey, on a colt, the foal of a donkey."* Zechariah 9:9.	This prophecy stipulates that the Jewish king will ride into Jerusalem on a colt. This prophecy was fulfilled when the Apostles *"...went and found a colt outside in the street, tied at a doorway. As they untied it, some people standing there asked, 'What are you doing, untying that colt?' They answered as Jesus had told them to, and the people let them go. When they brought the colt to Jesus and threw their cloaks over it, he sat on it."* Mark 11:4-7.
15.	*"Even my close friend, someone I trusted, one who shared my bread, has turned against me."* Psalm 41:9.	This is Judas Iscariot: *"When evening came, Jesus was reclining at the table with the Twelve. And while they were eating, he said, 'Truly I tell you, one of you will betray me.' ...Then Judas, the one who would betray him, said, 'Surely you don't mean me, Rabbi?' Jesus answered, 'You have said so.'"* Matthew 26:20-25.
16.	*"I told them, 'If you think it best, give me my pay; but if not, keep*	The 30 pieces of silver was a standard price to buy a slave. Still, it is unusual to specify that the money would be thrown into the

	it.' So they paid me thirty pieces of silver. And the Lord said to me, 'Throw it to the potter'-the handsome price at which they valued me! So I took the thirty pieces of silver and threw them to the potter at the house of the Lord." Zechariah 11:12-13.	House of the Lord and mention a potter. *"When Judas, who had betrayed him, saw that Jesus was condemned, he was seized with remorse and returned the thirty pieces of silver to the chief priests and the elders...So Judas threw the money into the temple and left. Then he went away and hanged himself. The chief priests picked up the coins and said, 'It is against the law to put this into the treasury, since it is blood money.' So they decided to use the money to buy the potter's field as a burial place for foreigners."* Matthew 27:3-7. Judas accepted 30 pieces of silver to betray Jesus, threw the money back into the Temple of the Lord, and hanged himself. The priests bought the potter's field with the money. These unusual prophecies of Zechariah were fulfilled.
17.	*"He was oppressed and afflicted, yet he did not open his mouth; he was led like a lamb to the slaughter, and as a sheep before its shearers is silent, so he did not open*	John the Baptist refers to Jesus as the Lamb of God: *"The next day John saw Jesus coming toward him and said, 'Look, the Lamb of God, who takes away the sin of the world!'"* John 1:29. When questioned by the Sadducees and Pharisees, Jesus remained silent; *"Then the high priest stood up and said to Jesus, 'Are you not going to answer? What is this testimony*

	his mouth." Isaiah 53:7.	*that these men are bringing against you?' But Jesus remained silent." Matthew 26:62-63.*
18.	*"My mouth is dried up like a potsherd, and my tongue sticks to the roof of my mouth; you lay me in the dust of death. Dogs surround me, a pack of villains encircles me; they pierce my hands and my feet. All my bones are on display; people stare and gloat over me. They divide my clothes among them and cast lots for my garment." Psalm 22:15-18.*	This prophecy declares, *"…they pierced my hands and feet"* and is a reference to crucifixion. The oldest known crucifixion was documented by the Greek Herodotus in 562 B.C.,[100] and this verse was written over 400 years before that. The psalmist described a manner of death (crucifixion) before it was even known! The *'pack of villains'* were the jeering people, including Pharisees and Sadducees. All of Jesus' bones were on display because he was naked. The *'…cast lots for my garment'* is rather specific. *"This garment was seamless, woven in one piece from top to bottom. 'Let's not tear it,' they said to one another. 'Let's decide by lot who will get it.'"* John 19:23-24. Yes, the soldiers did cast lots for Jesus' clothes.
19.	*"The righteous person may have many troubles, but the Lord delivers him from them all; he protects all his bones, not one of them will*	The comment about no bones broken is specific. *"Now it was the day of Preparation, and the next day was to be a special Sabbath… they asked Pilate to have the legs broken and the bodies taken down. The soldiers therefore came and broke the legs of the first man who*

---

[100] https://www.grunge.com/587858/history-of-crucifixion-explained/

	be broken." Psalm 34:19-20.	had been crucified with Jesus, and then those of the other. But when they came to Jesus and found that he was already dead, they did not break his legs." John 19:31-33. There are no accounts of any of Jesus' bones being broken.
20.	"He was despised and rejected by mankind, a man of suffering, and familiar with pain. Like one from whom people hide their faces he was despised, and we held him in low esteem... But he was pierced for our transgressions, he was crushed for our iniquities; the punishment that brought us peace was on him, and by his wounds we are healed." Isaiah 53:3-5.	This ancient prophecy was fulfilled through Jesus' life and crucifixion. Jesus was held in low esteem by the Pharisees and Sadducees. He was scourged, beaten, crucified, and pierced with a Roman spear. "He committed no sin, and no deceit was found in his mouth. ... 'He himself bore our sins' in his body on the cross, so that we might die to sins and live for righteousness; 'by his wounds you have been healed.'" 1 Peter 2:22-24.
21.	"But I am a worm and not a man, scorned by everyone, despised by the	The people stood watching, and the rulers sneered at Jesus. They said, "...He saved others; let him save himself if he is God's Messiah, the Chosen One." Luke 23:35.

	people. All who see me mock me; they hurl insults, shaking their heads. 'He trusts in the Lord,' they say, 'let the Lord rescue him. Let him deliver him, since he delights in him.'" Psalm 22:6-8.	This is another old prophecy that was fulfilled with Jesus on the cross.
22.	*"They put gall in my food and gave me vinegar for my thirst."* Psalm 69:21	This prophecy was fulfilled when Jesus was on the cross. He was offered wine mixed with gall: *"There they offered Jesus wine to drink, mixed with gall; but after tasting it, he refused to drink it."* Matthew 27:34. He was also offered wine vinegar: *"When some of those standing there heard this, they said, 'He's calling Elijah.' Immediately one of them ran and got a sponge. He filled it with wine vinegar, put it on a staff, and offered it to Jesus to drink."* Matthew 27:47-48. 'Posca' was an Ancient Roman drink made by mixing vinegar, water, and maybe herbs. It was the soldiers, the lower classes, and the slaves who drank posca. The Roman soldiers offered Jesus posca.

23.	*"'In that day,' declares the Sovereign Lord, 'I will make the sun go down at noon and darken the earth in broad daylight.'"* Amos 8:9.	Amos wrote his prophesies about 760 years before the birth of Jesus. *"From noon until three in the afternoon darkness came over all the land."* Matthew 27:45.
24.	*"He was assigned a grave with the wicked, and with the rich in his death, though he had done no violence, nor was any deceit in his mouth."* Isaiah 53:9.	As a poor carpenter, Jesus's body would have been put in a mass grave. But he was put in the tomb of Joseph of Arimathea, a rich man: *"As evening approached, there came a rich man from Arimathea, named Joseph, who had himself become a disciple of Jesus... Joseph took the body, wrapped it in a clean linen cloth, and placed it in his own new tomb that he had cut out of the rock."* Matthew 27:57-60.
25.	*"Therefore my heart is glad and my tongue rejoices; my body also will rest secure, because you will not abandon me to the realm of the dead, nor will you let your faithful one see decay."* Psalm 16:9-10.	Jewish bodies at the time of Jesus always decayed because the Jews did not adopt Egyptian embalming. Jesus' body did not decay: *"Fellow Israelites, I can tell you confidently that the patriarch David died and was buried, and his tomb is here to this day...Seeing what was to come, he spoke of the resurrection of the Messiah, that he was not abandoned to the realm of the dead, nor did his body see decay."* Acts 2:29-31.

AN ARGUMENT AGAINST BELIEVING THESE PROPHECIES

People might say, *"Well, of course these were fulfilled! Jesus and the Apostles knew about these prophesies and ensured that they were fulfilled."* Some of the prophesies involved others doing things to Jesus. For example, how do you force...

- Guards to cast lots for your clothes?
- Soldiers to beat you in the face so you are hardly recognizable?
- A soldier to stab you with a spear while you are defenseless on a cross without breaking any bones?

It doesn't make sense to believe that.

PART 5: ANALYSIS

An unaddressed issue is the dating of ancient biblical texts. A prophecy isn't a prophecy unless it was written before the event. It is critical that we explore this issue.

I asserted that these prophesies were hundreds to at least 1,000 years before Jesus was born. How do we know that this is true? Literary historians use the ancient text itself to date its creation. For example,

I used prophecies from the Old Testament book of Isaiah. He prophesied during the reigns of three Jewish kings of Judah: Uzziah, Ahaz, and Hezekiah (Isaiah 1:1). He was called to be a prophet when King Uzziah died (Isaiah 6:1), and Isaiah recorded the death of Sennacherib, a King of the Assyrian Empire. King Uzziah is a known historical figure and he died circa 740 B.C., and King Sennacherib died in 681 B.C. These dates show when Isaiah's book was written.

Two prophesies are from Zechariah, and the text dates itself by saying, *"In the eighth month of the second year of Darius..."* (Zechariah 1:1). Darius was the King of Persia and is another well-known historical figure. Similar examples occur in the writings of other ancient prophets in the Old Testament.

We can confidently accept that all the prophesies I listed were written before Jesus was born.

A second critical issue is the fulfillment of a prophecy. For example, here is a prophecy from Isaiah that I didn't use: *"For to us a child is born, to us a son is given, and the government will be on his shoulders. And he will be called Wonderful Counselor, Mighty God, Everlasting Father, Prince of Peace."* Isaiah 9:6. One might argue that other people could be called those names, such as perhaps King Solomon. However, the quote also describes Jesus and the prophecy was fulfilled in Him. That's the point.

A third issue is that the prophecies must be independent of each other. A prophesy written years earlier cannot influence a later one. The Old Testament authors indeed knew about earlier writings. However, the prophecies chosen are unique, so they are not like earlier ones.

Given the above, we can now conduct an experiment.

An Experiment

Examining 25 prophesies is an experiment. It is a random experiment with only two possible outcomes:

- Each prophecy was <u>not</u> fulfilled through the life of Jesus. We'll call this **Heads**.
- Each prophecy <u>was</u> fulfilled through the life of Jesus. We'll call this **Tails**.

'Not fulfilled through the life of Jesus' means that each prophecy was fulfilled through something else such as random chance, Karma, natural events, etc. For the sake of brevity, I'll call this 'other events.' Our null hypothesis is that <u>all</u> the prophesies I cited were fulfilled by other events and none through Jesus. Saying that 25 of 25 prophesies were fulfilled by other events is the same as getting 25 Heads when you flip a coin 25 times. Can other events explain the fulfillment of these prophecies?

This experiment is identical to flipping a coin because there are only two possible outcomes: Heads or Tails, and coin flip results conform to a binomial distribution.[101] We could flip a coin 25 times as an experiment and count the number of Heads. Normally, one would expect a combination of Heads and Tails in multiple coin flips because there is a 50% chance that each flip results in a Heads or a Tails. We'd then repeat this experiment thousands of times to calculate the probability of achieving 25 Heads with 25 coin flips. Again, 25 Heads in 25 coin flips mean all the prophecies were fulfilled by other events.

Doing that experiment thousands of times will take time, of course. We don't have to take that time! Instead, we can use the binomial distribution formula[102] to calculate the probability of getting 25 Heads in 25 coin flips. What is that probability? It is 0.00000002980 and is too small to be seen in the graph:

---

[101] Steel, R. and J. Torrie. 1980. Principles and procedures of statistics. McGraw-Hill Publishing Company, New York. 633 pp.
[102] https://en.wikipedia.org/wiki/Binomial_distribution

Binomial Distribution N=25

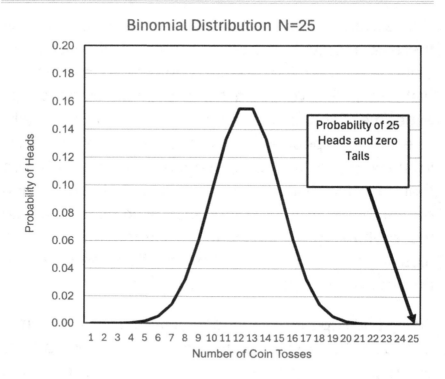

Probability of 25 Heads and zero Tails

STATISTICAL SIGNIFICANCE IN SCIENTIFIC PUBLICATIONS

What does a probability of 0.00000002980 mean in the scientific community? The gold standard for significance is a probability (alpha level) of 0.05, meaning there is only a 5% chance that the null hypothesis is correct. Sometimes, a scientist wants to be extra cautious and uses an alpha level of 0.01... only a 1% chance that the null hypothesis is correct. A scientist would report the actual probability level (p) from a statistical analysis and compare it against the preset alpha level.

For example, we did an experiment that measured the impact of different planting dates and tillage systems on the abundance of an insect pest in peanut fields.[103] The null hypothesis was that neither planting date nor type of tillage would affect the abundance of this insect. We discovered that late planting increased the abundance of the insect pest in peanut fields (p<0.01). This is a statistically significant result. We <u>rejected</u> the null hypothesis that the planting date didn't affect the abundance of this insect. Farmers could plant peanuts early and mostly avoid getting this insect in their fields.

Let's apply this approach to the prophecies and their probability of p=0.00000002980. Again, the null hypothesis is that <u>all</u> the prophecies were fulfilled by other events (e.g., 25 Heads in 25 coin flips). The probability of this occurring by other events is <u>far</u> smaller than needed in scientific publications. In plain language, a p=0.00000002980 means:

Less than one chance in 33 million

That is far smaller than a 5% (5 out of 100) or even a 1% (1 out of 100) chance that the null hypothesis is correct. Scientists are ecstatic when they see a probability that is this small because they have found something significant and publishable.

---

[103] Mack, T. and C. Backman. 1990. Effects of two planting dates and three tillage systems on the abundance of lesser cornstalk borer (Lepidoptera: Pyralidae), other selected insects, and yield in peanut fields. J. Econ. Entomol. 83(3): 1034-1041.

STATISTICALLY SIGNIFICANT, By Tim Mack

This minuscule probability causes us to <u>emphatically reject</u> the null hypothesis that all 25 prophecies happened by other events. At least one of those prophecies must have been fulfilled by Jesus' life. The prophecies were NOT fulfilled by other events but through Jesus.

If you are a non-believer, you must believe that the prophecies happened by other events and accept this extremely small probability. Who would do that? A statistically inclined unbeliever might attack this mathematical argument by saying, *"Hey, wait a minute! It's also true that the probability of 25 Tails is the same as 25 Heads!"* If 25 Heads mean that all were fulfilled by other events, then 25 Tails mean that Jesus fulfilled all of them. This is statistically correct. It is also statistically true you get a mixture of Heads and Tails when you flip a coin repeatedly. Even if Jesus only fulfilled SOME of the prophecies, then He is the Son of God. If you want to dismiss all 25, you are back to a less than one in 33 million chance.

In addition to this mathematical analysis, I showed <u>evidence</u> that Jesus fulfilled all 25 prophecies. An unbeliever must show us evidence that refutes these 25 prophecies and that they were fulfilled by other events. I don't know how anyone could do that. And that's just the beginning of problems for an unbeliever.

There are <u>109 unique prophecies</u> that the unbeliever must refute. In his book, 'God's Plan for the Ages,' Pastor David Reagan noted that, *"The Bible contains more than 300 prophecies about the First Coming of Jesus. Many of these are repetitious. When the duplicates are removed, the total number of prophecies which Jesus fulfilled is 109—all of which were literally fulfilled."*[104] He documented how each one was fulfilled and listed 0 (zero) prophecies that weren't fulfilled.[105] The probability of all 109 of the unique prophecies being fulfilled by other events is 0.00000000000000 0000000000154074.

This isn't 1 in a million, 1 in a billion, 1 in a trillion, or even 1 in a quadrillion. It is:

Less than one chance in 649,000,000, 000,000,000,000,000,000,000,000

In other words, the probability of the prophecies fulfilled exclusively by other events is so infinitesimally small that only a fool would believe it. The fulfillment of prophecies is the closest thing to proof that Jesus is the Son of God.

---

[104] Reagan, D. 2020. God's Plan for the Ages: The Blueprint of Bible Prophecy. Lion and Lamb Ministries, McKinney, TX. 383 pp.
[105] Reagan, D. 2017. Christ in Prophecy Study Guide. Lion and Lamb Ministries, McKinney, TX.150 pp.

SUMMARY

1. Sufficient data support the conclusion that the Old Testament prophecies were written before Jesus was born.
2. The prophecies are unique and are thus independent of each other.
3. There are 109 unique prophecies in the Old Testament that Jesus fulfilled. The probability that just 25 prophecies were fulfilled by other events is less than 1 in 33 million, far smaller than needed in scientific publications.
4. The probability that 109 prophecies were fulfilled by other events is infinitesimally small.
5. The prophecies were NOT fulfilled by other events.

Believe.

PART 6: COMPREHENSIVE SUMMARY

Below is a compilation of all the historical, medical, geological, astronomical, medical, prophetic, and mathematical data analyses. It is a compelling list.

1. The New Testament has been transmitted from disciple to student, and those men all describe the death and resurrection of Jesus.

2. Outside data sources affirm Jesus' death and resurrection and concur with Polycarp and Irenaeus.

3. Another confirmation comes from the scribes' precise methods of creating copies of ancient documents. In the scientific world this is extremely careful and exact handling of data. Further, the data were verified by other people (i.e., Rabbis). This care is impressive.

4. The Codex Sinaiticus, dating from 300 to 399 A.D., is amazingly close to the King James Version, dating from 1611 A.D. It is a telling example of how the New Testament has been handed down from generation to generation.

5. There are thousands of ancient copies of the New Testament and their uniformity strengthens the hypothesis that it has been accurately handed down to us.

6. The New Testament was written soon enough after Jesus' death that false information is unlikely.

7. What we see today is what was originally written.

8. Many ancient cities, temples, and other stone structures have been found, verifying locations in the New Testament.

9. Archeological findings confirm the existence of Caiaphas, Pontius Pilate, James the brother of Jesus, and four Roman Emperors mentioned in the New Testament.

10. All the archeological discoveries related to the New Testament confirm the biblical text and none contradict it.

11. The archeological evidence continues to grow as new discoveries are made.

12. The 'counterculture' narrative featuring women in the New Testament is unlikely to be fictional. Further, people's flaws in the New Testament are a sign of authenticity.

13. Writings from outside sources reinforce the New Testament narrative.

14. Jesus very likely suffered from hypovolemic shock caused by a tremendous number of wounds. He probably had a pericardial effusion and perhaps a pleural (i.e., lung) effusion. He died from all his wounds and loss of blood.

15. A Roman soldier ensured that Jesus was dead by piercing him with a spear, probably in the heart. The pericardial sac (or the pleural sac) ruptured, causing clear plasma and blood to drain from the wound.

16. There is evidence for the earthquake described in the Bible.

17. The sky went dark for hours. It is astronomically impossible for it to have been a normal solar eclipse.

18. The guards did not dare fall asleep for fear of execution. No Jew would unwrap Jesus' dead body and remove it from the tomb because it is sacrilegious to do so. It is illogical to unwrap a dead body and then fold the headpiece.

19. Jesus died.

20. Hundreds saw someone claiming to be Jesus for over a month.

21. Of the more than 500 people who saw this person, no one denied that it was Jesus. There are no stories of recanting inside or outside of the New Testament.

22. Jesus appeared to his half-brother James, who would have recognized if it wasn't Jesus.

23. All Apostles except John were executed for their beliefs and some of the executions were brutal. None recanted. Hundreds of early Christians were persecuted for their beliefs and none recanted. This is compelling evidence.

24. The Apostles' behavior changed 180 degrees from timidity to fearlessness when preaching the Gospel due to seeing Jesus after he died.

25. Collectively, these data affirm the New Testament account that Jesus rose from the dead.

26. Sufficient data support the conclusion that the Old Testament prophecies were written before Jesus was born.

27. The prophecies are unique and are thus independent of each other.

28. There are 109 unique prophecies in the Old Testament that Jesus fulfilled. The probability that just 25 prophecies were fulfilled by other events is

less than 1 in 33 million, far smaller than needed in scientific publications.

29. The probability that 109 prophecies were fulfilled by other events is infinitesimally small.

30. The prophecies were NOT fulfilled by other events.

This comprehensive analysis shows that Jesus is the Son of God. He lived, was tortured and died, and rose from the dead. It also means that everything that he said is true.

Now What?

The text in this book is black, and the pages are white. Similarly, your choice is black or white. You are faced with only two possibilities:

1. The God of the Bible is real, or
2. The God of the Bible is not real.

You've seen historical, archeological, astronomical, geological, medical, prophetic, and even mathematical evidence that Jesus is the Son of God.

Choose wisely for your eternal soul's sake.

"If you declare with your mouth, 'Jesus is Lord,' and believe in your heart that God raised him from the dead, you will be saved. For it is with your heart that you believe and are justified, and it is with your mouth that you profess your faith and are saved." Romans 10:9-10. You should do this if you now believe. It is important and you can do this even if you are the only one who can hear you say those words.

If you have accepted Jesus, then this is a wonderful day! A thousand years from now, your soul (your memories, emotions, the essence of who you are) will be <u>alive</u> and happy.

"Very truly I tell you, whoever hears my word and believes him who sent me has eternal life and will not

be judged but has crossed over from death to life." John 5:24.

You will also eventually have a new body, as the Book of Revelation describes. You will experience the incredible views, activities, and wonders of Heaven.

To ensure that you'll stay the course as a Christian, there are next steps that a new believer normally takes.

READ THE BIBLE: It isn't enough to declare that you believe in God. You also must read God's Word to know what He is telling us to do, how to act, and how to live our lives. You can read any Bible but pick one you want to read. You won't want to read it if it is hard to read. There are so many to choose from! The New International Version is an accurate translation, and the English Standard Version is similar. Both are readable. There are many Bibles but I recommend the English Standard Bible Study Guide. This is a suitable place to start, and it is my daily Bible. It has over 20,000 study notes and more than 240 illustrations. The illustrations are detailed and helpful.

Either buy a commentary or select a Bible with explanatory text. The goal is to read and understand the biblical verses. Reading the Bible isn't about reading words; it is about understanding them. You need a Bible that helps you know the history, geography, and other cultures in the Bible (See image). Such information is essential to understanding the biblical text.

Understanding the Bible

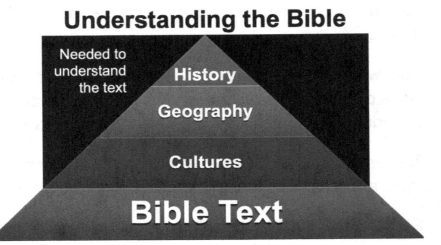

Try to read at least two chapters daily- one from the Old Testament and one from the New Testament. Suppose you also read the explanatory paragraphs and study the maps and illustrations. In that case, this should take you about ½ hour each day. Does the hypothetical daily chart below of how someone spends most days describe you?

TASK	HOURS
Job	9
Rest & sleep	8
Family time; Unwind	3
Shop; Chores; etc.	2.5
Hobbies & Sports	1
Praying; Studying the Bible	0.5

It does for many of us. Devoting ½ hour a day to God seems minimal. You certainly should be able to do that.

If you can do more, then do so. Praying multiple times per day- even one-sentence prayers- is rewarding. Don't forget to ask God what He wants of you.

BE WITH OTHER CHRISTIANS: As a new Christian, you'll need support. You need to be with other Christians who can help you grow and commiserate with you in times of stress. It is too easy to backslide into a fuzzy, non-committing 'belief' in God. *"Yes, God is real,"* you might say to yourself. *"The sun rises in the east and sets in the west,"* you might also say. These are academic beliefs and are without emotional content. You must have more than belief; you must have a <u>living relationship</u> with God.

It is important that you know Jesus, but it's more important that <u>Jesus knows you</u>. How will He know you if you never converse with him? That includes asking him questions and asking for advice. Jesus isn't an ATM machine where you only go to him when you need something.

An effective way to be with other Christians is to join an online or face-to-face Bible study group. You can learn about the Bible, meet new people, and ask questions simultaneously. If you are an introvert, you can text questions to one of your Christian friends. Don't go it alone.

FIND A GODLY CHURCH AND ATTEND IT: This is hard. The Apostle Paul said, *"I know that after I leave, savage wolves will come in among you and will* *not spare the flock. Even from your own number men will arise and distort the truth in order to draw away disciples after them."* Acts 20:29-30. Satan has been using people to twist scripture for thousands of years.

Find a church that believes the following:

1. There is only one God.
2. Jesus is fully God and fully human.
3. Jesus died for our sins, and he rose from the dead.
4. The Bible doesn't need to be modernized.

Find a church that accepts all of these and you should grow in Christ. That's what you want!

Does the Bible Need to be Modernized?

People will say that the Bible wasn't designed for today's times and needs updating. Others will say that the Bible describes patriarchal societies and thus doesn't match today.

Is this true? Aren't the "old times" in the Bible so different that it doesn't apply to today?

The "old times" in the Bible were much harsher than today, so the Bible's verses should apply just as well today as they did back then. There were brutal, pagan societies such as the Babylonians, Assyrians,

Moabites, Amalekites, Amorites, and others. These cultures worshiped Asherah, a fertility goddess; Ba'al, the 'Storm God;' and Chemosh, 'The detestable god of Moab' (1 Kings 11:7). Chemosh worshippers engaged in human sacrifice. Some ancient peoples worshipped Molech (also called Molek), who demanded child sacrifice. The chosen mother gave her baby to the priest, who put the infant onto the bronze arms of a scorching hot Molech statue, and the infant died screaming in front of the worshippers. Thankfully, we don't have any religion like that today.

The 'old times' were indeed harsh and the Old Testament has eye-opening examples of this. For example, the Assyrian Empire conquered what is the northern half of Israel today. This militaristic empire lasted about 700 years,[106] conquered almost all the modern-day Middle East, and was a brutal and repressive regime. They skinned people alive and made large stone tablets (i.e., ancient billboards) displaying their cruelty to people visiting their cities.[107]

Slavery was rampant in the "old times" as the Persian Empire, the Assyrian Empire, the Babylonian Empire, and the Roman Empire embraced slavery. Slaves comprised up to 25% of the population of Rome. Human rights were few.

---

[106] https://en.wikipedia.org/wiki/Assyria
[107] https://listverse.
com/2016/12/07/10-horrors-of-being-invaded-by-the-assyrian-army/

Sexual practices haven't changed much in the past 3,000 years. The "old times" included male and female prostitutes, bestiality, and men who became eunuchs.[108] Homosexuality and cross-dressing were described in Deuteronomy, which is over 3,000 years old. The practice of abortion is more than 4,000 years old.[109]

The seven deadly sins (Lust, Gluttony, Pride, Greed, Sloth, Wrath, Envy) were prevalent in the 'old times' and still are today. We are far more technically and medically advanced today, but human nature hasn't changed.

In ancient times, no U.S. governmental support programs such as Welfare, the WIC Program, Medicaid or Medicare, food stamps, or Social Security existed. People worked until they died. Medical knowledge was scant, and there were no antibiotics, vaccines, or internal surgeries to remove cancers. If the Bible was applicable during harsher times, it is applicable today. It seems to me that the people described in the Old and New Testament had a tougher life than me, so it doesn't make sense that the Bible needs to be modernized or re-interpreted.

Yes, it was a patriarchal society when the New Testament was written. Women back then did more

---

[108] https://www.britannica.com/topic/eunuch
[109] https://truthout.org/articles/abortion-is-as-old-as-pregnancy-4-000-years-of-reproductive-rights-history/

than we may think, though. A Proverb written more than 500 years before Jesus was born describes a wife of noble character: *"She considers a field and buys it; out of her earnings she plants a vineyard."* Proverbs 31:16. So, she has her own earnings, decides to buy land, and then plants a revenue-producing crop on it. It may surprise you to read how independent she was. She made her own money and decided how to spend it. We also see a woman who helps the poor and needy, speaks with wisdom and faithfully instructs her children (Proverbs 31:10-31). Women in the 'old times' worked extremely hard and deserved respect, as women do today.

"As for God, his way is perfect: Lord's word is flawless; He shields all who take refuge in him." Psalm 18:30. Some people today will not like this message. You see, Christianity is exclusive. People will be excluded from Heaven and go to Hell. The Bible doesn't say that everyone goes to Heaven. It says the opposite repeatedly. The people that aren't likely to accept this message are those who worship themselves.

SELF-WORSHIP

In 2021, Self-Worship was listed as the world's fastest-growing religion.[110] Jesus is the Son of God and we shall put no other gods before Him, including

---

[110] https://www.thegospelcoalition.org/article/self-worship-booms/

ourselves. It is too easy to fall into self-worship these days because much of what we see on TV, hear on the radio, and view on the internet is about self. Someone wants to sell us something, or we hear a song about making our own choices, or we watch a TV program where someone like us succeeds against all odds. Self-Worship is all about 'me'. God isn't about 'me'.

Self-worship has common phrases that we hear almost daily:

SELF-WORSHIP PHRASES	BIBLE VERSES
Follow Your Heart	*"It is the Lord your God you must follow ..."* Deuteronomy 13:4.
Live Your Truth	*"I am the way, and the truth and the life..."* John 14:6.
You Only Live Once	*"Whoever believes in me, though he die, yet shall he live."* John 11:25 ESV.
To Find Yourself, Look Within Yourself	*"You will seek me and find me, when you seek me with all your heart."* Jeremiah 29:13.

As you can see, the Bible teaches us a quite different view of the world. Paul says in Ephesians 4:22-24, *"You were taught, with regard to your former way of life, to put off your old self, which is being corrupted by its deceitful desires; to be made new in the attitude of your minds; and to put on the new self, created to be like God in true righteousness and holiness."*

There is an old saying…it is okay for the boat to be in the sea, but it is not okay for the sea to be in the boat. Don't let the worldly sea get into your Christian boat.

You have a purpose now- to share the Gospel. That purpose will exist for as long as you live. How should we act, then, in this world? A great answer to that question is in Titus 2:7-8 ESV, which says, *"Show yourself in all respects to be a model of good works, and in your teaching show integrity, dignity, and sound speech that cannot be condemned, so that an opponent may be put to shame, having nothing evil to say about us."* We have something that no one can take away…but we can give it away. That something is integrity. Don't give your integrity away because it is hard to get back.

BEWARE OF PROSPERITY THEOLOGY

This is a fast-growing movement in Protestantism today.[111] This denomination teaches that Jesus died for our sins, including the 'sin' of poverty. Prosperity Theology teaches that you won't get seriously ill or be poor if you have enough faith.

---

[111] https://research.lifeway.com/2023/08/22/prosperity-gospel-beliefs-on-the-rise- among-churchgoers/

Who doesn't want health and wealth? This is an easy sell. All that we must do is pray and donate money, and we will be healthy and rich. But we must beware of such teaching: *"For the time will come when people will not put up with sound doctrine. Instead, to suit their own desires, they will gather around them a great number of teachers to say what their itching ears want to hear."* 2 Timothy 4:3. Preaching what people want to hear is a sign of a false prophet.[112]

Being healthy and wealthy isn't what Jesus or his Apostles preached. Jesus said, *"No one can serve two masters. Either you will hate the one and love the other, or you will be devoted to the one and despise the other. You cannot serve both God and money."* Matthew 6:24. Jesus talked extensively about money and warned how one can inappropriately worship it. Being wealthy isn't automatically bad; what you do with the wealth matters. Zacchaeus is a good example because he didn't spend all his money on possessions for himself. *"But Zacchaeus stood up and said to the Lord, 'Look, Lord! Here and now I give half of my possessions to the poor, and if I have cheated anybody out of anything, I will pay back four times the amount.'"* Luke 19:8.

Jesus' Apostles spent years with him. Paul was a tentmaker and kept working while he witnessed to

---

[112] https://www.biblestudytools.com/bible-study/topical-studies/10-ways-we-can-recognize-a-false-prophet.html

others. The Apostles could heal the sick and cast out demons, but none were rich. Jesus' Apostles would have been financially rich if the Prosperity Theology were correct.

You can't buy healing or wealth by donating to Prosperity churches. God's blessing can't be bought. God's grace has saved us: *"For it is by grace you have been saved, through faith—and this is not from yourselves, it is the gift of God— not by works, so that no one can boast."* Ephesians 2:8-9.

The Apostle Paul had the power to heal others: *"God did extraordinary miracles through Paul, so that even handkerchiefs and aprons that had touched him were taken to the sick, and their illnesses were cured and the evil spirits left them."* Acts 19:11-12. Yet, he couldn't heal himself! *"Therefore, in order to keep me from becoming conceited, I was given a thorn in my flesh, a messenger of Satan, to torment me. Three times I pleaded with the Lord to take it away from me. But he said to me, 'My grace is sufficient for you, for my power is made perfect in weakness.'"* 2 Corinthians 12:7-9. God can certainly bless us when we pray and ask for help. His blessing might take the form of healing or money, but it could also take other forms. God is good all the time. Please be careful about Prosperity Theology.

Don't Worship a False God

Imagine having a cell phone app called 'Create-a-God' where you can create the kind of God you want to worship. What kind of God would you create? Would the God be male, female, both, neither, or non-binary? What color would your God be? Would your God be loving, caring, and forgiving? Would your God ever be angry, and would your God ever punish someone? Would you create a God that puts souls into Hell?

People create their own personalized god all the time. It is so easy to do this! They create a god (lowercase 'g') that matches what they want to believe. The god they make isn't the God of the Bible, of course. Pastor Phil Ware noted, *"We live in an age when people want to mix the contents of many mystical faiths and spirituality into the boiling pot of a self-made pseudo-Christian religion because they added a little Jesus to their mix."*[113] We can't make God conform to our beliefs; instead, we should make our beliefs conform to God.

Some people today want half of God, the loving half. They want a loving and caring divine being. God is undoubtedly loving! The Apostle John wrote, *"And so we know and rely on the love God has for us. God is love. Whoever lives in love lives in God, and God in them."* 1 John 4:16. We also read about Jesus'

---

[113] https://www.verseoftheday.com/en/08192024/

STATISTICALLY SIGNIFICANT, By Tim Mack

answer to a question from a Pharisee. *"But when the Pharisees heard that he had silenced the Sadducees, they gathered together. And one of them, a lawyer, asked him a question to test him. 'Teacher, which is the great commandment in the Law?' And he said to him, 'You shall love the Lord your God with all your heart and with all your soul and with all your mind. This is the great and first commandment. And a second is like it: You shall love your neighbor as yourself. On these two commandments depend all the Law and the Prophets.'"* Matthew 22:34-40 ESV. Yes, God is love! We should be all about love. A Christian should have the light of Christ shining through us so brightly that others notice us. We become that light by reading, believing, and living God's words in the Bible.

But God isn't only love. Some people ignore the Old Testament because they don't like the God in it. He is the same God in both the Old and the New Testaments. If someone ignores the Old Testament, then he or she missed all 25 of the prophecies I mentioned in this book! The Old Testament is filled with rich stories, useful lessons, and instruction about the nature of God. For example, God <u>describes himself</u> in the Old Testament when Moses received the Ten Commandments, *"And he passed in front of Moses, proclaiming, 'The Lord, the Lord, the compassionate and gracious God, slow to anger, abounding in love and faithfulness, maintaining love to thousands, and forgiving wickedness, rebellion and sin. Yet he does*

STATISTICALLY SIGNIFICANT, By Tim Mack

not leave the guilty unpunished;'" Exodus 34:6-7. God says He is slow to anger, but He didn't say He is never angry. He also says that He 'does not leave the guilty unpunished.'

Nothing is wrong with the God of the Old Testament. God didn't attend anger management classes during the 400 years between the Old and New Testaments. He is loving and caring, sometimes angry and always just. He will punish sin. There are things that He thinks are an abomination and things that He hates.

These are an abomination to God:

- False Gods (Exodus 34:13-14).
- Child sacrifice, fortune telling, sorcery, inquiring of the dead (Deuteronomy 18:9-13).
- Ungodly sexual relationships (1 Timothy 1:8-11).
- Wickedness (Proverbs 15:9).
- False teachers (Titus 1:10-16).

These are things that God hates: *"There are six things that the Lord hates, seven that are an abomination to him: haughty eyes, a lying tongue, hands that shed innocent blood, a heart that devises wicked schemes, feet that are quick to rush into evil, a false witness who pours out lies, and a person who stirs up conflict in the community."* Proverbs 6:16-19.

What about Jesus? Isn't Jesus just about love? Well, not really. He angrily overturned the money lenders' tables in the Temple and made a *"whip of cords"* John 2:13-15. He told the Pharisees that they were a *"brood of vipers"* and asked them how they could escape being sentenced to Hell (Matthew 23:33). Jesus also said, *"Do not suppose that I have come to bring peace to the earth. I did not come to bring peace, but a sword. For I have come to turn 'a man against his father, a daughter against her mother, a daughter-in-law against her mother-in-law—a man's enemies will be the members of his own household.'"* Matthew 10:34-36.

Ignoring the God of the Old Testament is separating Him from the New Testament Jesus. This splits the Holy Trinity or Triune God. Jesus is inseparable from God. Jesus said, *"I and the Father are one."* John 10:30. The Apostle John wrote perhaps the most beautiful words in the Bible about Jesus, who is the Word. *"In the beginning was the Word, and the Word was with God, and the Word was God. He was with God in the beginning. Through him all things were made; without him nothing was made that has been made. In him was life, and that life was the light of all mankind."* John 1:1-4.

We see that Jesus was with God from the beginning and made all things...including the Old Testament. Jesus made this point himself when he asked, *"If you believed Moses, you would believe me, for he wrote about me. But since you do not believe what he wrote, how are you going to believe what I say?"* John 5:46-47.

The Bible teaches us that there is only one way to Heaven. *"Jesus answered, 'I am the way, and the truth, and the life. No one comes to the Father except through me.'"* John 14:6. He is the only way to Heaven. That may sound harsh to you. But remember that Jesus was beaten twice, scourged, struck with rods, crucified, and then stabbed with a Roman Spear. He bore horrific punishment and then died. Jesus endured all that for nothing if there were other ways to God. Pastor Greg Laurie noted, *"That is why it is insulting to God to suggest that all religions are true and that whatever belief system you adopt will get you to Heaven if you are sincere. If that were the case, do you think that God the Father would have allowed His Son to suffer like He suffered, both in Gethsemane and on the cross?"*[114]

The Bible doesn't say to accept everyone <u>and</u> their sins. A verse used to justify this viewpoint is **"Do not judge, or you too will be judged. For in the same way you judge others, you will be judged, and with the measure you use, it will be measured to you. 'Why do you look at the speck of sawdust in your brother's eye and pay no attention to the plank in your own eye? How can you say to your brother, 'Let me take the speck out of your eye,' when all the time there**

---

[114] https://harvest.org/resources/devotion/the-cup-of-suffering/.

is a plank in your own eye? You hypocrite, first take the plank out of your own eye, and then you will see clearly to remove the speck from your brother's eye.'" Matthew 7:1-5. It doesn't say, 'and then ignore the speck in your brother's eye,' it says that we should take the speck from our brother's eye. We should correct others in sin when their theology or behavior is wrong. We should do this because we love them and don't want them to go to Hell. Pastor Billy Graham wrote, *"Yes, God is loving and compassionate. But He is also absolutely holy and pure, and because of that He is the Judge who will someday bring His full wrath to bear on those who refuse to repent."*[115]

There is an <u>eternal</u> cost to creating your own personalized god. Millions of people today have done this. What will happen to them after they die? In Matthew 7:21-23 we read, *"Not everyone who says to me, 'Lord, Lord,' will enter the kingdom of heaven, but only the one who does the will of my Father who is in heaven. Many will say to me on that day, 'Lord, Lord, did we not prophesy in your name and in your name drive out demons and in your name perform many miracles?' Then I will tell them plainly, 'I never knew you. Away from me, you evildoers!'"* It would be appalling to hear *"Away from me"* after years of devoting ourselves to A god but not THE God.

---

[115] Graham, W. 2017. Hope for Each Day daily devotional—September 3rd.

We don't choose what God is like; God does.

We don't determine what is moral and just; God does.

We don't decide what is sinful; God does.

We should read the Old and New Testaments and worship God with respect and awe (Hebrews 12:28-29). How should we act? We should *"Love the Lord your God with all your heart and with all your soul and with all your mind and with all your strength."* Mark 12:30, and *"Love your neighbor as yourself."* Mark 12:31. Loving someone means that you support them, help them, and correct them when they are doing something wrong.

I also like what the Apostle Paul wrote: *"Love is patient, love is kind. It does not envy, it does not boast, it is not proud. It does not dishonor others, it is not self-seeking, it is not easily angered, it keeps no record of wrongs."* 1 Corinthians 13:4-5. To me, this describes what we should aspire to be every day.

Please worship the God of the Bible and not a Create-a-God.

The Body, the Soul, and the Spirit

The differences between the body, the soul and the spirit are confusing to new Christians, so I thought you'd appreciate a discussion of this topic. We read, *"For the word of God is alive and active. Sharper than any double-edged sword, it penetrates even to dividing soul and spirit, joints and marrow; it judges the thoughts and attitudes of the heart."* Hebrews 4:12.

What is the difference between the body, the soul, and the spirit, and what do those differences mean to Christians? One way to think about this is to imagine a three-story house:

The ground floor is the body and is the physical part of us. We all have bodies and know how they grow, develop, and age.

The house's second floor is higher than the first, and the second floor is the soul. It is who we are...our memories, experiences, emotions, and personality.

We see these attributes in several Bible verses. For example, *"Why, my soul, are you downcast? Why so disturbed within me? Put your hope in God, for I will yet praise him, my Savior and my God."* Psalm 42:11. We also read about getting along well, which is related to our personality, *"Dear friend, I pray that you may enjoy good health and that all may go well with you, even as your soul is getting along well."* 3 John 1:2. Then, we learn about 'refreshing the soul,' which is reviving or reanimating our soul, *"The law of the Lord is perfect, refreshing the soul."* Psalm 19:7.

Everyone has a soul, just like everyone has a body. The souls of believers who have died are in Heaven; we know this because we read about them being there. For example, the martyrs asked God how long they would wait until they were avenged: *"When he opened the fifth seal, I saw under the altar the souls of those who had been slain because of the word of God and the testimony they had maintained. They called out in a loud voice, 'How long, Sovereign Lord, holy and true, until you judge the inhabitants of the earth and avenge our blood?' Then each of them was given a white robe, and they were told to wait a little longer, until the full number of their fellow servants, their brothers and sisters were killed just as they had been."* Revelation 6:9-11.

The highest floor of this three-story house is the spirit. It is much smaller than the other two floors because the gate is narrow to Heaven and wide to Hell (Matthew 7:13-14). The spirit is the subconscious part of us that connects with God. Christians receive the Holy Spirit of God when they believe. For example, Jesus described what would happen to the Apostles when they received the Holy Spirit, *"But you will receive power when the Holy Spirit comes on you; and you will be my witnesses in Jerusalem, and in all Judea and Samaria, and to the ends of the earth."* Acts 1:8.

This spirit intercedes for us with God, *"In the same way, the Spirit helps us in our weakness. We do not know what we ought to pray for, but the Spirit himself intercedes for us through wordless groans. And he who searches our hearts knows the mind of the Spirit, because the Spirit intercedes for God's people in accordance with the will of God."* Romans 8:26-27.

Only believers receive this spirit, and nonbelievers die without the Spirit: *"As the body without the spirit is dead, so faith without deeds is dead."* James 2:26. People without the spirit don't have their names written in the Book of Life and will be cast into the lake of fire after they die (Revelation 20:12-15).

American General George S. Patton wrote, *"So as through a glass, and darkly The age long strife I see..."*[116] Indeed, we do see daily strife. But that will change after we die, *"For now we see only a reflection*

---

[116] https://en.wikipedia.org/wiki/Through_a_Glass%2C_Darkly_(poem)

as in a mirror; then we shall see face to face. Now I know in part; then I shall know fully, even as I am fully known." 1 Corinthians 13:12. What a wonderful thing it will be to see God!

May God bless you today. Keep reading and keep praying. Finally, I ask that you don't be like I was. I grew too slowly as a Christian and didn't develop a genuine relationship with God until more than 30 years after first believing. I first believed in God when I was young, and the woman who became my wife witnessed to me. My slowness hampered my personal growth and my relationship with others. I sincerely regret some things that I said and did. Over the years, I became more conscientious about reading the Bible, and a major negative event in 2015 brought me face-to-face with my flawed nature. I was baptized in 2019. I could have been a much better person if I had tried harder to be a committed Christian when I first believed. Be better than me.

Good Resources

I thought you might appreciate a list of good Bible study resources. There are many such resources and this is not an exhaustive list.

DAILY VERSES: It is helpful for people to receive a verse in their email inbox each day. Here are sites that do this:

1. Biblegateway.com.[117] This is a daily verse without commentary. It is easy to read.
2. Verseoftheday.com[118] by Pastor Phil Ware. This is a daily verse with commentary and you can listen to it if you wish. This daily devotional is read by over ½ million people each month. I read it every day.
3. BibleStudyTools.com. Verse of the Day.[119]
4. Word Alert cell phone app. This is an IOS application that you download to your iPhone. It has a daily Bible verse.
5. Inspirations cell phone app. This is an IOS application that you download to your iPhone. It has a verse plus a particularly good commentary.

DAILY DEVOTIONALS: There are hard- and soft-bound books with a daily Bible verse and commentary. I will mention three that are best sellers:

1. 'Hope for Each Day,' by Pastor Billy Graham. This is an excellent devotional.
2. 'Experiencing God, Day-by-Day,' by Pastors Henry T. Blackaby and Richard Blackaby. This daily devotional is thought-provoking.
3. 'Truth for Life,' by Pastor Alistair Begg. Pastor Begg is an excellent speaker and writer who sticks to the biblical text.

---

[117] https://www.biblegateway.com
[118] https://www.verseoftheday.com
[119] https://www.biblestudytools.com/bible-verse-of-the-day/

BIBLE STUDY GUIDES: You can find Bible concordance websites online that are free, such as BibleHub,[120] and photos of places in the Bible from Bibleplaces.[121] The Blue Letter Bible website[122] will show you the original language for each verse, Strong's dictionary, and commentaries for each verse.

BIBLICAL KNOWLEDGE SITES: There are online resources for you, such as www.biblestudytools.com, www.gotquestions.org, and others. A good site for learning about the archeology of the Bible is biblearcheology.org, from the Associates for Biblical Research.

YOUTUBE SITES: Be careful here because there are so many false prophets on the internet. Compare everything that you hear with the biblical text. If it doesn't fit, then stop watching or listening. This also holds for TV shows, movies, and songs. This is such a quickly changing field that I am uncomfortable recommending websites. Instead, I suggest you study the theology of someone who preaches or teaches the Bible on YouTube. The YouTube site should be good if the theology matches the Bible's teachings. Trust, but verify.

---

[120] https://www.biblehub.com

[121] https://www.bibleplaces.com

[122] https://www.blueletterbible.org

Acknowledgments

I humbly stand on the shoulders of giants. There are so many that have influenced me and paved the way for this book: Josh McDowell, Frank Turek, J. Warner Wallace, Phil Ware, Billy Graham, Dick Gilbert, David Jeremiah, David Reagan, John McArthur, John Piper, Allen Parr, D. James Kennedy, Charles Stanley, the Associates for Biblical Research and others. I am thankful for each of them. I also thank the reviewers of early drafts of this book.

The #1 thing that I am thankful for is that Jesus saved me.

About the Author

Tim Mack has a B.A. in Biology from Colgate University and a M.S. and Ph.D. in Entomology from The Pennsylvania State University. He was an assistant professor, associate professor and professor at Auburn  University; Department Head, Director, Assistant Dean, and Associate Dean at Virginia Tech; Graduate Dean at Georgia Southern University; and Graduate Dean & later Dean of Extended Studies at Indiana University of Pennsylvania. Tim produced 247 refereed and non-refereed publications during his career. He won two national teaching awards and was a newspaper columnist for several years. He is retired and trying to live up to his name, which means *'honoring God'* in Greek.

Tim thanks each one of you for reading this book. **You are important**- don't ever forget that. Please remember the <u>message</u> of this book, not the messenger. God helped Tim to write it.

"So Jesus said to the Jews who had believed him, 'If you abide in my word, you are truly my disciples, and you will know the truth, and the truth will set you free.'"

John 8:31-32 ESV.

Printed in the United States
by Baker & Taylor Publisher Services